The
Connell Guide
to

The
American
Civil War

by Adam Smith

Contents

How unified was the South? 82

How unified was the North? 87

When and how did the war end? 93

Why did the South lose? 99

Conclusion 103

Introduction

The war in North America between 1861 and 1865 is estimated to have cost three quarters of a million lives. Few societies in world history have lost a higher percentage of their military-aged men in battle than did the white South. Unsurprisingly, its scars have lain deep on the American soul – especially so in the former Confederacy.

Yet the war's historical significance is based on more than just the scale of the violence. It is *the* great American story. "I am large, I contain multitudes," wrote Walt Whitman, the great poet of American democracy, but the war through which he lived, nursing devastatingly injured soldiers, contains even more "multitudes" than him. It is a story that can be told in a million different voices; it contains heroism and cowardice, craven injustice and heart-warming redemption; above all, it is the great American story because it seems to matter so much.

It was the "crossroads of our being", in the words of Shelby Foote, a historian who found popular fame through an extraordinarily successful 1991 TV documentary made by Ken Burns. Foote implied that all American roads led to and from the great conflict of the 1860s. In so many ways, this is surely true. Whether the issue is the continuing struggle for racial equality, the scope of govern ment, the place of violence in American life or the potential for war to achieve noble ends, the paths the United States has taken can indeed be traced back to those brutal battles 150 years ago.

If the war was a crossroads, one road not taken was disunion: the break-up of the United States and, as has often been imagined, the death of free government everywhere. In the view of Abraham Lincoln, the man whose figure looms more than any other over this great crisis, the American Union was the "last, best hope of earth". Speaking at Gettysburg, Pennsylvania in November 1863, at the ceremony to dedicate a cemetery to those who had died in the three-day battle earlier that year, Lincoln claimed that at stake in the conflict was not just the territorial integrity of his nation but the question of whether government of, for and by "the people" would "perish from the earth".

These universal claims were not just the chauvinism of a nationalist American leader. They were more interesting than that because they were echoed around the world, by men and women who knew America only through what they had heard and read. When the news of Lincoln's assassination reached western Europe some 12 days after the event, the impact was extraordinary. The meeting of "condolence" in Hyde Park in London was the largest anyone could recall. Even obscure towns in rural France sent petitions praising the slain president to the American minister in Paris.

Lincoln's death mattered because America mattered. Consequently, the war was followed with obsessive interest in Europe and Latin America.

While some foreigners saw the conflict primarily in terms of its impact on trade and manufacturing (the American South was the near-monopoly provider of raw cotton) and conservatives could not hide their *schadenfreude* at the apparent failure of an impudent young experiment in democratic rule, many identified wholly with the Union cause. The western world was still living in the shadow of the failure of the 1848 European revolutions. Would the one great hope of liberal, popular movements – the "Great Republic of the West" – now also collapse?

The struggles in Virginia and Tennessee were seen as the latest front in an ongoing global contest between despotism and democracy. As Lincoln was aware, it mattered not just for Americans but for "the whole family of man". In 1865, Professor E.S. Beesly, a left-leaning historian at University College London, argued that "with the defeat of the Confederacy, a vast impetus has been given to Republican sentiments in England". America was a "standing rebuke to England. Her free institutions, her prosperity, the education of her people, the absence of a privileged class, are in too glaring a contrast with our own position to be forgiven."[*] This perception that their cause had been the cause of freedom has provided Americans – those who wanted it – with what the poet and novelist Robert Penn Warren, a Southerner born exactly half a century after the guns fell silent, called a "treasury

[*] *Bee-Hive* April 29, 1865.

of virtue". The Civil War, one of the most destructive conflicts in western history, was immediately imagined as a "Good War", reaffirming the fundamental "goodness" of America.

Since Warren coined the phrase in the 1960s, the "virtue" Americans could find in the war has been seen less through the prism of perpetuating democracy (which at the time meant government by white men) and more through the moral accomplishment of ending slavery. Some four and half million men, women and children were no longer legally regarded as property after the Thirteenth Amendment to the Constitution came into effect in the aftermath of the war. But self-congratulation on that undoubted advance in human freedom should be tempered by two considerations. First, the end of slavery was only the first in a long and twisted path toward equality; and, second, abolition was the result of contingency as much as intent, and happened because it was expedient as much as right.

Slavery, its eventual abolition and its legacy are inextricable from any discussion of the war's causes, course and consequences. But although slavery is in some ways a very American story (it fuelled the new nation's spectacular economic growth), the United States was far from the only place to see a revolutionary transformation in labour relations in the 19th century. Wage labour, once rare, became the norm. Across the New World property in humans was abolished – in the British, French, Portuguese,

Spanish, Dutch and Brazilian empires. And elsewhere in the world, too, other forms of unfree labour came to an end, whether serfdom in Russia and Prussia or other forms of slavery in the Middle East, Africa and Asia. In this sense, the "great American story" of the Civil War should not solely be told with reference to the United States: it is part of a global story as well.

What makes the Civil War so important, even to us now, is what it tells us about the great struggles and the big historical forces that have shaped the modern world. The ending of slavery as part of a series of other emancipations is one example. So

HOW WAS THE HISTORY OF THE WAR WRITTEN IN THE FIRST 50 YEARS AFTER 1865?

The first generation to write histories of the war were those who had served. Not surprisingly, they tended to emphasise the higher purposes for which men had died. For those on the wining side this meant the survival of the Union. The ending of slavery was not ignored altogether, but it was subsidiary to the main achievement of the conflict, which was keeping together the United States, with its supposedly unique commitment to liberty. African Americans and a few former abolitionists kept alive the memory of the struggle for black freedom, of course. Frederick Douglass gave powerful speeches in the post-war years calling on the nation not to walk away from its sacred pledge to the freedmen.

By the time of the 50th anniversary, something like a cross-sectional consensus on how to remember the war had emerged. By removing slavery from the story and focusing

too is the importance of nationalism – the idealisation of the nation-state (by both North and South) as the vehicle through which to advance great ideals. And ultimately, the Civil War, by vindicating "free government" – as Lincoln and millions of others saw it – played a powerful role in validating liberal and democratic ideas, with huge consequences for the even greater military struggles of the 20th century. If the Civil War is the crossroads of America's being, it is also, in a different sense, one of the major crossroads over which the world has travelled in its journey to the present.

Crossroads, by their nature, force people to

entirely on national reunification, white Northerners and white Southerners found a shared way to recognise each others' valour and celebrate the United States's unprecedented strength. The war that the United States launched against Spain in 1898 was an important staging post in this process of national reconciliation as Northerners and Southerners fought together against a common foe.

In the aftermath of the First World War, the Lincoln Memorial was built in Washington DC, a monument not to the moral cause of emancipation but to the nation.

"In this temple," runs the inscription carved into stone above the massive recumbent statue, "as in the hearts of the people for whom he saved the Union, the memory of Abraham Lincoln is enshrined forever."

It would be an exaggeration to say that by this point Lincoln had become a universal hero – he remained hated by many in the South – but, by casting him as a nationalist and not an emancipator, the process of canonising him as a unifying figure was well under way. In parallel, Robert E. Lee became a symbol of nobility and heroism, a reluctant rebel whom Northerners, too, could revere. ∎

make choices. The Civil War made people choose: between loyalty to the North or the South; between the perpetuation of slavery or its abolition, making harder some fudged compromise between the two. It is too easy for us, with the benefit of hindsight, to see this great crisis and its outcome as inevitable. How could tension between an anti-slavery North and a slaveholding South *not* end in war, we might think? And how could that war then *not* end with abolition? Was it ever really possible that the United States, so dominant a force in world history ever since, might have broken apart?

But of course no one at the time knew what was about to hit them. While slavery had been abolished in the British Empire in the 1830s, twenty years later it was more firmly established in North America than ever before, the cotton grown by enslaved labour a major source of wealth for some of the most powerful people in the country. There was every reason to imagine that slavery, notwithstanding the rising anti-slavery movement, had become simply too important for it to be abolished. And unlike in Britain, where ultimately Parliament had the authority to abolish slavery, the federal nature of the American constitution meant that no Congress or president in Washington could do the same. The best hope of those who wished to see a United States free of slavery seemed to be that if they could exclude slaveholders from the national government and then surround the slave states with a cordon of freedom, pressure could eventually be

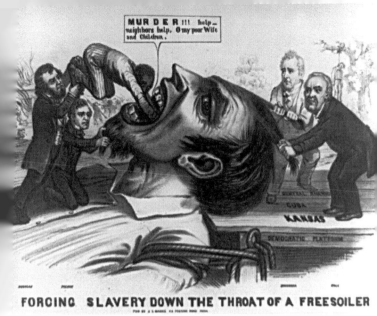

FORCING SLAVERY DOWN THE THROAT OF A FREESOILER

A cartoon from 1854 depicting a giant free soiler being held down while Stephen Douglas pushes a black man down his throat.

exerted that would lead slave states to embrace some sort of gradual abolition, sweetened – as emancipation had been in the United Kingdom – with a massive bribe to slaveholders to compensate them for the loss of what was, legally if not morally, their human property.

Such an eventuality was wished for and prayed for, but there were few concrete reasons to believe it would happen. There was, however, one circumstance in which all historical precedent and most legal argument suggested that the Federal government *could* legitimately forcibly emancipate slaves and even formally abolish the laws that made slavery sustainable. It was the circumstance in which, back in the 1770s, the Royal Governor of Virginia, Lord Dunmore, had issued a proclamation promising freedom to enslaved people who demonstrated their loyalty to the King: war.

Was slavery the cause of the war?

No serious historian would contest this, although a majority of the US public in opinion polls reject the claim. The popular unwillingness to accept that slavery was at the root of the conflict is partly a reaction to the efforts made by educationalists and academics since the 1960s to place it there. The insistence of slavery's centrality feels, to some Americans, like a liberal conspiracy to impose on the Civil War a narrative that will prop up present-day efforts to tackle racial inequality, or, still worse, an attempt to make white people feel "guilty".

Such is the continuing toxicity of race in American society that the Civil War can never escape its politics. But there are also two arguments against the proposition that slavery caused the war: most white Southerners, including most of those who fought for the Confederacy, were not slaveholders; and most white Northerners were certainly not abolitionists. Neither of these facts, in themselves, however, show that slavery was not the cause of the war. They merely illustrate what is definitely true: that the war was no straightforward fight between humane abolitionists on the one hand and slaveholders on the other. Our challenge is to understand how slavery came to be such a difficult problem that it led to war, even though the abolitionist movement remained small.

The stubborn fact is that, simply put, had slavery not existed there would have been no war. Alternatively, had slavery been distributed evenly over the United States, with all of the states having a similar investment – legally, financially, culturally and emotionally – in slavery, there would have been no war either. As everyone in America understood at the time, slavery created a culture in the South that was discernibly different from that which existed in the free states to the North. It also created a different kind of politics, and ensured that Southern economic development was on a distinctively different trajectory from that of the North. As Abraham Lincoln put it in 1865, reflecting on the origins of the conflict: "All knew that [slavery] was *somehow* the cause." The question, then, is *how*?

The economic problem was in a way the most obvious, although also more complicated than it has seemed since in some respects slavery bound together Northern merchants and manufacturers with Southern cotton planters. But at the same time, there was a clash between powerful Southern economic interests and those of the rest of the country.

The political problem was that slaveholders seemed increasingly to threaten the republican freedom of white Americans by demanding more and more Federal control, and to shut out the opportunities otherwise available to free white labourers in the west. In this sense the conflict became both one over the nature of American democracy and at the same time a fight over access to resources – basically, land.

The cultural problem could also be expressed as a moral problem. It was that slavery – since it was not just a particular sort of economic interest but was also a claim about the nature of humanity – generated distinct cultures in North and South. This point can be exaggerated, but it cannot be denied: the religious awakening of the early part of the 19th century affected both sections, but only in the North did it foster an evangelical reform movement that generated mass sympathy for the plight of the enslaved.

When we talk about what caused the Civil War, we are really talking about three separate questions. First, what caused the sectional tension between North and South that made war possible? Second, why did first seven and then eventually a further four slave states leave the Union in 1860-61? And third, why did the North respond to secession with the use of massive state violence to hold the nation together?

Slavery is at the heart of the answer to the first question, although historians debate exactly *how* and *why* slavery created those tensions. As for the second question, defence of slavery was quite explicitly the reason given by the seceding states themselves. The answer to the third question is complicated, but even though most Northerners definitely did not say they were fighting to end slavery (they said they were fighting for the Union), they all understood that since slavery was – in the contemporary phrase – "the tap-root of the rebellion". Ultimately only by uprooting it could the nation live.

How different were North and South on the eve of war?

As measured by religious affiliation, language, or culture, not significantly. Even the economic differences can easily be exaggerated: most people in both the free states and the slave states were farmers. Americans in all sections revered a common moment of national origin and shared a republican sensibility which prized the equality and independence of free (white) men and was deeply suspicious of concentrations of power.

But there were differences – in the higher rate of urbanisation, industrialisation and immigration in the North – that were a direct consequence of the reliance of the South on slave-produced cotton. It was this distinction – one that had been growing over the preceding decades – that underlay the increasing *perception* of difference.

From the time of the Revolution onwards, there were differences in constitutional interpretation as well, with Southerners more likely to argue that the Federal Union was a voluntary compact among sovereign states (who could therefore leave if they wished), and Northerners more likely to imagine their national origins in the popular endorsement of "the people" as a whole. But even this was traceable to slavery. The nightmare of being trapped in an abolitionist republic was one that haunted leading Southerners from the outset.

Southerners came to view "Yankees" as moralising money-grubbers: the "roundheads" to the Southerners' "cavaliers". This stereotype had at least a little foundation in the pattern of emigration to the colonies in the 17th and 18th centuries, with East Anglian Puritans dominating settlement in New England while Southern English royalists were more influential in Virginia. Regional differences, however, overlay this sectional divide. By 1800, a separate "Western" identity was already visible, and within the South the Appalachian Mountains fostered a very distinct culture of poor, self-reliant white farmers with far fewer slaves than the wealthier lowland areas.

Transportation revolutions – roads, canals and, above all, railroads – added a further transformative element to this mix. After the building of the railroads from the big east coast cities into the

Ohio valley the great farming regions of the Midwest were connected to eastern markets rather than, as before, being dependent on having to float their produce slowly down the Mississippi River to New Orleans.

This economic change reoriented sectional identities, binding the Midwest to the Northeast rather than the South. More generally, industrialisation and urbanisation meant that the free states were developing a more diverse and – as they themselves continually pointed out – more dynamic and entrepreneurial economy.

By 1860, most Northerners, then, still worked on the land as did most Southerners. But those Northern farmers were more conscious than ever before of what they imagined (not inaccurately) to be the greater opportunities for economic advancement available in the free states, without competition from slave labour, or the looming presence of "aristocratic" slaveholders. Convinced of the superiority of free labour, Northerners wanted to ensure that there would be no barriers to the widely held ambition to expand into the fertile farmland of the west.

Did the Constitution play a role in the development of the crisis over slavery?

Yes. It is fundamental to understand this. The United States was (and is) a Federal republic. Congress was not sovereign in the same sense as Parliament was in Britain, or an autocratic ruler in some other European countries. The Tsar of Russia could (and did) simply issue an edict to free the serfs. No such thing was possible in the United States.

Federalism means that sovereignty is divided. In a few areas (such as setting the level of tariffs to be levied against imported goods, running a national post office or declaring war) the Federal government in its various branches had sole authority. In most other areas – including who could vote, criminal law, property law and therefore the laws of slavery – it was the states which had the power. This meant that when Southern slaveholders set up a new federation, the "Confederate States of America", in 1861, it was, relatively speaking, easy to do because slaveholders already controlled the state governments – the entities where most of the decisions affecting people's lives were made. And it meant that almost everyone agreed that there was literally no legal, constitutional way that the

Federal government could abolish slavery *within a state*. This "Federal Consensus", as it has been dubbed, was shared even by people who hated slavery.

Moreover, the Constitution, in various direct ways, protected slavery. For example it offered guarantees – backed up by legislation – that enslaved people who escaped into a free state would be returned to slavery under Federal authority, whatever local laws might say to the contrary. It also gave an advantage to slaveholding states in the allocation of votes in the Electoral College that elected the president, and in the apportionment of members of the House of Representatives, by determining their voting strength not just on the basis of free people but on the basis of three-fifths of the enslaved population as well. Slaveholders had it both ways: the Constitution recognised slaves as property (hence they had to be returned if they escaped) but recognised that they were in some sense people, too, by allowing them to be counted (albeit at a discounted rate) for the purposes of apportionment.

This was why the abolitionist William Lloyd Garrison called the Constitution a "Covenant with death" and an "agreement with Hell".* In saying this, he was agreeing with more moderate voices that the Constitution protected slavery. The political ostracism that resulted in him using such

* *Boston Daily Atlas*, July 6, 1854.

language illustrated why this mattered so much: the Constitution was regarded as literally sacred.

Most big political issues in the United States become constitutional issues. Today, the debate about gun control is inseparable from the Supreme Court's interpretation of the meaning of the Second Amendment to the Constitution, which refers in passing to the right of the people to "bear arms". Issues like gay marriage or abortion are never just discussed on their own merits but in terms of whether they are constitutional or not. In the same way, 19th-century Americans spent a great deal of time arguing about slavery in relation to the Constitution.

Since no one could argue that the Federal government had the power to abolish slavery, the debate centred on whether Congress had the power to exclude slavery from areas where it did have control: in Federal Territories – places, generally in

WHY DID SLAVERY EXIST IN THE SOUTH BUT NOT IN THE NORTH?

It had not always been so: at the time of the American Revolution, there were slaves in Boston townhouses as well as in Virginian tobacco fields.

But the states north of what came to be known as the Mason-Dixon line gradually abolished slavery in the 30 years after the Revolution. The South did not – not least because Virginia in particular (then by far the largest slave state) had so large a population of enslaved people that men like Thomas Jefferson who favoured emancipation in the

the west, which had not yet been officially admitted into the Union as states and so were in a sort of transition stage, with a locally-elected legislature but a governor appointed by the president and all decisions affecting the territory ultimately overseen by Washington.

The debate on the Federal government's authority over slavery in the Territories was not just about where slavery existed, or whether it could or should spread. It was also about the fundamental character of the Republic. Was it a basically free Union with slavery recognised as an exception to the general rule of freedom only in a few states? Or was it basically a slaveholding Union, in which a few states nevertheless excluded slavery?

---

abstract worried about the practical consequences.

And then, with the demand for raw cotton growing as the Industrial Revolution took off in Britain, slavery suddenly became highly profitable.

By 1860, the South was more dependent than ever on its system of forced labour. The development of the world economy in the mid 19th century was dependent on slavery, with raw cotton playing a similar role to oil in the 20th century as the commodity that drove growth.

Far from being a *Gone With the Wind*-style throwback to a semi-feudal pre-industrial time, the Southern slave economy was therefore modern, highly capitalist, completely integrated into global trade patterns, and generated hundreds of millions of dollars in profit. ■

Why did Northerners oppose slavery?

We may assume, from our own perspective, that Northerners saw slavery as a moral outrage intolerable in their own country. There were some who thought like this, to be sure. There were always principled, humanitarian opponents of slavery in the United States, often driven by religion. Inspired by the success of the abolitionist movement in Britain, reformers sought to remove slavery just as they sought to remove other sins – abuse of alcohol,

HOW DID SLAVEHOLDERS EXERCISE POWER IN THE UNITED STATES BEFORE THE WAR?

The most basic requirement for maintaining a slave system is having the government on your side. If you want to buy, sell, invest and hold a human being as "property", you have to be sure that the courts, legislature, police, and all the authority of the state are going to back you up. If not, your personal safety is under threat (slave insurrections were a constant source of fear for the white South), and your financial investment (billions of dollars by 1860) vulnerable.

Slaveholders had been dominant among the Founding Fathers – of the early presidents, Washington, Jefferson, Madison, and Monroe were all slaveholders from Virginia; they established a beachhead in Washington that was not breached until 1860.

Apart from John Adams (1797-1801) and his son John Quincy Adams (1825-1829), every single president from Washington to Lincoln was

for example, or Sabbath-breaking.

The fear and indignation such reformers caused in the South was one of the primary reasons for secession. The explosive impact of Harriet Beecher Stowe's novel *Uncle Tom's Cabin* (1852) testifies to the power of anti-slavery ideas to move tens of thousands of people. But the history of abolitionism does not in itself explain Northern hostility to slavery. To understand that, we need to grasp how slavery came to seem a threat to the freedom of white Northerners.

One of the main grievances that 18th-century colonists had against Britain was that the

---

either a slaveholder or a strong supporter of slavery. Since the president appoints the members of the Supreme Court it followed that the Court was also pro-slavery. And since one of the pro-slavery provisions of the Constitution was to apportion members of the House of Representatives, and since the Senate represented states equally irrespective of their population size, the South – despite its smaller population – was over-represented in Congress too.

The world's first mass political party, the Democrats, was also, in practice, a means by which the South could exercise Federal power. The party stood for westward expansion and the equality of white men and it attracted support in all parts of the country. Although many of its northern supporters were not actively pro slavery (and a few were actively anti-slavery) the party functioned to keep Southern leaders in power in Washington.

It is no coincidence that only when the Democrats failed to maintain their hold on national power – in the 1860 election – did slave states secede from the Union, triggering the war. ■

government in London, attempting to keep the peace with Native American tribes, tried to prevent white settlement west of the Appalachian Mountains. As soon as the US became independent, that restriction was lifted. Westward movement – the constant search for new, cheap, fertile land – was fundamental to Americans' sense of what made their republic a true land of opportunity. The "safety valve" of western lands was what prevented the overcrowding and class tensions that beset the Old World. Consequently, as new land was added to the Union, Northerners wanted to be sure that it would be open to this American Dream of self-improvement.

But if slavery was present, could a white man prosper? Probably not. After a massively successful war against Mexico in the 1840s, the territorial size of the US was increased by a third: California, with its newly-discovered gold, together with most of today's Arizona, New Mexico, Utah, Nevada and Colorado came into American hands. This provoked a great battle over whether slavery should be banned.

A compromise was, reluctantly, reached in 1850, but then the whole issue was opened up again by the Kansas-Nebraska Act of 1854. Probably the most consequential piece of legislation ever passed by Congress, this Act removed a 34-year-old ban on slavery in Kansas and Nebraska: territories that had been first acquired in the Louisiana Purchase of 1803 but which had not yet been politically

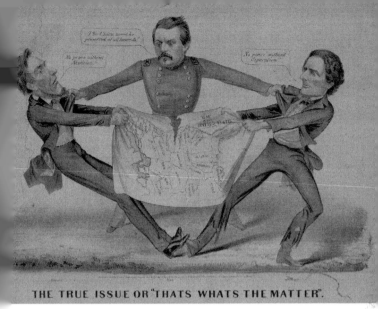

THE TRUE ISSUE OR "THATS WHATS THE MATTER".

Pro-McClellan cartoon portraying Lincoln's former Commanding General mediating between the extreme positions of Lincoln and Jefferson Davis.

organised or settled. It was now clear to increasing numbers of Northerners that slaveholders, not content with simply running their slave systems where they currently existed, wanted to expand, and in doing so to block Northerners from expanding their free labour society.

In other ways, too, slaveholders seemed to threaten white freedom. A much-strengthened Fugitive Slave Act, passed in 1850, bypassed Northern courts and contained a provision that any white Northern man could be impressed into a slave patrol to recover a runaway slave. Never mind the violation of the rights of the enslaved, this was a violation of white people's freedom. As a rising politician in Illinois, Abraham Lincoln, was to put it, the question was becoming whether the country would become "all slave, or all free". It was harder and harder to sustain a middle-ground position.

Northerners overwhelmingly disliked the idea of slavery. They did not want to reintroduce it among themselves. The very idea was the antithesis of the ideal of freedom that they held dear. Yet, overwhelmingly, they were racist too and they certainly did not want to live in a bi-racial democracy. They were also, most of them, innately suspicious of moralising reformers pursuing per-fectionist ideals. Abolitionists were not popular people.

Northerners also knew very well that constitutionally there was no way that slavery

"REVISIONIST" HISTORIANS AND THE "NEEDLESS WAR" THESIS

Modern historians, writing since the Civil Rights movement of the 1950s and 1960s, tend to take the antislavery movement seriously. In this, they follow the standard line of the first half-century of writing about the Civil War, which took for granted what had seemed obvious to the combatants: that slavery was the basic cause, that it had been the result of an "irrepressible conflict" between the sections and that, for all the bloodshed, the war had been fought for noble ends.

In contrast, "Revisionist" historians writing in the 1920s and 1930s found it hard to imagine a legitimate cause that could justify the cost of the conflict. Influenced by the

could be banned in the Southern states unless those states themselves wanted to ban it (and there was precious little sign of that). But what they could not accept was the "nationalisation" of slavery: it was one thing for slavery to be the exception to the general rule of freedom; it was quite another for those propositions to be reversed. Yet that was exactly what Southerners, by the mid-1850s, were demanding.

The infamous Dred Scott decision by the Supreme Court (1857) ruled that Congress could no more ban slavery from any US territory under its jurisdiction than it could from a state. Rather than slavery only being allowed to exist under the protection of state laws, while the nation as a whole protected liberty, as Northerners had

---

carnage of the First World War, they questioned whether the Civil War need have been fought at all. Two of the most influential Revisionists, Avery Craven and James G. Randall, argued that the war was needless because there were no important differences separating the sides.

Slavery had reached its "natural limits" within the United States, limits bound by climate, which meant that it was not going to spread into the new western territories whatever the laws might say.

This was very similar to the argument made back in the 1850s by Stephen Douglas, who urged fellow Northerners to focus on the pragmatic question of whether slavery was expanding, not on the legal-philosophical question of whether it could or should. For Randall the phony arguments over slavery ("an imaginary negro in an impossible place") were the "amazingly thin" basis on which "antagonistic emotions" had been whipped up by power-hungry politicians. The war, Randall

always imagined, the Supreme Court now ruled, in effect, that the only places where slavery could be banned were territories within states. And even a state's ability to ban slavery was limited and vulnerable. How long, Northerners asked, before a slaveholder could move to New York or Massachusetts and be able to remain there with his human "property" fully protected by the central government?

In the face of such rulings and legislation, even moderate, self-described "conservative" Northerners were appalled. They were facing a fully orchestrated revolution by slaveholders (or the "Slave Power" as it was now often known).

summed up, "could have been avoided, supposing of course that something more of statesmanship, moderation, and understanding, and something less of professional patrioteering, slogan-making, face-saving, political clamoring, and propaganda, had existed on both sides".*

This Revisionist perspective was discredited by two developments: the Second World War, which revived faith in a "good war" that could accomplish moral purposes, and the Civil Rights Movement. The revolution in racial attitudes that accompanied the latter dramatically altered historians' accounts of the war. In this context, Revisionists' unwillingness to accept the sincerity of the anti-slavery movement seemed morally obtuse.

While their books are now rarely read, aspects of the Revisionists' argument have continued to be influential. In recent years, historians have come to appreciate the importance of Randall's

Why was Lincoln elected in 1860?

Lincoln was the candidate of the new Republican Party and was only on the ballot in the free states. He won a majority in the Presidential Electoral College despite polling less than half of the national popular vote because he won a majority in almost all the free states and so scooped all their votes. Since there were more free states than slave states, this was sufficient for Lincoln to win.

Yet five years earlier the Republican Party had not existed. Its rise was the proximate cause of secession. The Republican Party was the means by which the North asserted, for the first time since

---

perception that sectional politics was highly emotional. We can get only so far in analysing the road to war if we just stress material conflicts of interest or even principled ideological conflicts. We need also to try to understand how fear, anger and indignation limited or spurred political action.

There are some historians who have been labelled "neo-Revisionists" because they do not accept that fundamental differences between two separate sections led ineluctably to conflict. An example is Michael F. Holt who (*unlike* the Revisionists) accepts that slavery was the fundamental cause of the war, but who argues (*like* the Revisionists) that to understand why war came about, we also need to understand how politicians exacerbated the crisis by pandering to their sectional electorates. ■

* J. G. Randall, *The Civil War and Reconstruction* (Boston: D. C. Heath, 1937), vii.

the Revolution, its ability when sufficiently united to control the Federal government, or at least its executive branch. It was the manifestation of what had long been an underlying reality: the South was a minority. This was the very thing that slaveholders, feeling their property to be acutely vulnerable, could not tolerate. And so the war came.

Southerners had long feared the emergence of a Northern sectional party – rightly, because by the 1850s they were decisively outnumbered. Any political movement that could sweep the North would then have the votes to control the House of Representatives and the Electoral College that chose the president. Before the rise of the Republican Party this had never happened – previous sectional parties had never managed to eclipse other parties with a cross-sectional support base. So how did the Republicans manage their unprecedented success?

Central to the story of the war, the party has attracted a great deal of scholarly attention. The main question has been whether it was more the cause of sectional antagonism or the consequence of it. The modern debate about this began with a hugely influential book published in 1970 by Eric Foner. Its title, *Free Soil, Free Labor, Free Men*, was a Republican slogan – one that Foner argued perfectly captured the blend of anti-slavery moralism, belief in free labour and aspirational self-interest that was the secret of the Republicans' success. For Foner, what mattered was not so much the *moral* aspects of slavery as its perceived threat to the *material* interests of Northerners.

In contrast, Michael Holt is probably the most influential of the historians who argue that the Republicans rose so quickly because of astute leaders who realised the political expediency of emphasising the threat to Northerners. They invoked the concept of "Slave Power" – the very phrase conjuring up the idea of a vast Southern conspiracy to corrupt the liberties of the North. Holt does not dispute that there was an underlying sectional conflict, but he emphasises the role of other divisive political issues, such as anxiety about immigration, in undermining the old party system and therefore creating the political space in which a new, explicitly pro-Northern party could operate. More recently, James Oakes, in *Freedom National* (2013), has returned to an older view that underpinning the Republicans was a genuine desire to contain, stigmatise and ultimately abolish slavery.

What all these historians agree on is that a major break point in Northern politics came with the passage through Congress of the Kansas-Nebraska Act of 1854. The bill had the ostensibly uncontroversial purpose of creating territorial government in the land to the west of Illinois. This was territory that had been part of the United States for half a century but had been barely settled by European Americans. Now, a combination of increasing settlement and the desire to build a railroad to connect the new state of California with the east, necessitated Kansas and Nebraska's "organisation".

The controversy arose because this was the last remaining part of the North American continent from which slavery had been banned under the terms of the Missouri Compromise (1820). But in order to support the bill's passage, Southern senators demanded that the status of slavery be redetermined by a vote of the local settler population. To millions of Northerners, including many who had never considered themselves anti-slavery before, this was a betrayal of a sacred promise that Kansas and Nebraska would be open to the free settlement of poor white men. More than that, it seemed to be evidence that the government was in the hands of a sinister, "aristocratic" Slave Power. The leading Northern Democrat, an old sparring partner of Lincoln's from Illinois, Stephen Douglas, was the bill's author and with a debatable degree of enthusiasm he endorsed the vote as the price to be paid for his overarching aim of expansion. In doing so, he split his own party and generated a ferocious Northern reaction that would lead some of his former Democratic colleagues to join in a new Republican Party.

"The North is Awake!" went the opening words of a Republican campaign song in the 1856 presidential election. If the party could unite the North, it could capture enough Electoral College votes to win the presidency even without having any support at all in the South. They didn't manage this in 1856; hapless Pennsylvania Democrat James Buchanan won instead. But in the coming few years the new party built support further as the South demanded even greater protection for its slave "property". And in 1860, with Lincoln as their nominee for the presidency, the Republicans won by positioning themselves as the best defenders of Northern liberty against the threat from the Slave Power. Their argument was that it was no longer a matter of needing to understand the legitimate concerns of the South in order to maintain sectional harmony: if the Union was to become a predominantly slaveholding republic, as the South now explicitly advocated, the promise of freedom would be fatally tarnished.

To Northerners, the bigger picture was the global struggle between democracy and despotism. It had been fought out in Europe in 1848, when revolutions had shaken France, Hungary and the German and Italian states. In America, Republicans thought, Southern slaveholders were the despots, trying to impose an undemocratic and unrepublican set of values on the nation, and they had to be resisted.

The Republicans' platform had a clarity about it that their opponents lacked. They would oppose the extension. (In practice, under pressure, Republicans fudged this commitment, but they made it, nonetheless, with no equivocation.) They drew support from voters who had supported the old Whig party (now moribund) and the Democratic Party. A widespread anxiety about corruption also tarnished the ruling party, paving the way for a supposedly new kind of politics to be ushered into power in 1860.

Anti-slavery Northerners welcomed Lincoln's election as a decisive break with the past. The patrician Bostonian Charles Francis Adams, son of former president John Quincy Adams, was elated that "the great revolution has actually taken place" and that "the country has once and for all thrown off the domination of the slaveholders". In the South, the so-called "fire-eaters", who had been campaigning for secession for years, appeared to have been prescient. Lincoln, like the rest of his party, believed slavery was *wrong*. To the leaders of Southern society, this was enough to persuade them that the Federal government, once safely dominated by people like themselves, had fallen into the hands of their enemies – irrevocably so, since the rising population of the free states meant that their Electoral College advantage would only increase. "The election of Lincoln," wrote one Southern politician, "has placed *our* necks under *their* heels."[*]

* Quoted in Morrison, *Slavery and the American West*, p. 257.

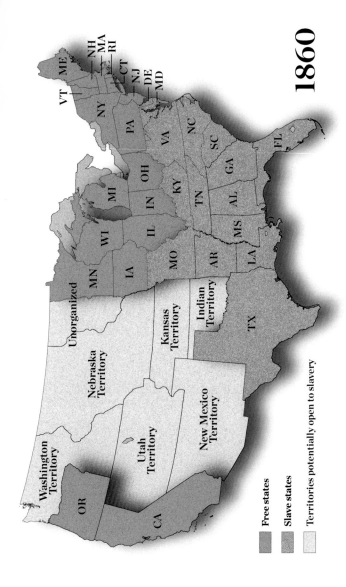

1860

VT
ME
NH
MA
RI
NY
CT
NJ
DE
MD
PA
OH
VA
NC
MI
IN
KY
SC
WI
IL
TN
GA
MN
IA
MO
AL
MS
AR
LA
Unorganized
Nebraska Territory
Kansas Territory
Indian Territory
FL
Washington Territory
Utah Territory
New Mexico Territory
TX
OR
CA

Free states

Slave states

Territories potentially open to slavery

35

ABRAHAM LINCOLN

Slightly stooping, with his over-size limbs never seemingly entirely in control, and his immensely sad eyes with that redeeming twinkle of humanity, Lincoln is a visually familiar figure in American culture even today. To an extent too infrequently recognised, the way in which the Civil War is remembered has been shaped by the views we ascribe to him and by his words.

Since the Civil Rights revolution placed race once again at the centre of the American story, Lincoln has been seen as the embodiment of the war's redemptive purpose. In him, white and black Americans alike have a figure to embody the hope of racial equality. When Martin Luther King came to Washington in 1963, a hundred years after the Emancipation Proclamation, to speak of his dream of ending racism, he did so from the steps of the Lincoln Memorial, and invoked the "Great Emancipator" in whose "shadow we stand".

As the Founding Fathers have become tarnished by their slaveholding (Jefferson's status will never be the same after DNA tests proved his sexual exploitation of his slaves), Lincoln – a founding father by proxy, though a generation removed – has become even more vital to the national imagination. He was the man who, in his own, ever-quotable words, saved the Union, this "last, best hope of earth", in such a way as to make it "forever worthy of the saving".

The real, live Lincoln did just enough to make such invocations plausible. He was not, by 21st-century standards, a campaigner for racial justice. But he was consistent in his view that not only was slavery wrong but that black people were just as entitled as anyone else to labour freely. He was born to subsistence farmers in 1809, in a log cabin in the then frontier state of Kentucky. Despite having virtually no formal education, he became a leading lawyer in Springfield, Illinois, and a prominent state politician.

A natural sceptic, he faced constant rumours of being a non-believer – a serious charge in such a Protestant society. Even so, he acquired the trappings of bourgeois respectability, aided by marriage to the daughter of a Kentucky slaveholder. Lincoln was born at just the right and time and place to experience, through hard work and luck, a very different life from his father (or, for that matter, most of his relations). Rapidly changing communication, technology and commerce in an expanding society enabled him to join the white-collar ranks of a new bourgeoisie.

After one term in Congress in the late 1840s, his political career seemed over and he returned to a legal career. But, like many others, he felt the Kansas-Nebraska Act was a challenge that had to be faced. In a speech in Peoria, Illinois, in 1854 Lincoln expressed the shame and anger so many Northerners felt at the expansion of slavery. "Our republican robe is soiled and trailed in the dust," he declared. "Let us repurify it. Let us turn and wash it white, in the spirit, if not the blood of the Revolution."

Over the next six years he campaigned against the perceived aggrandisement of the Slave Power and the complicity of some Northern politicians in the subversion of the principles of the republic. He was never an abolitionist: his aim was not to destroy slavery in short order, but simply to cordon it off, to re-assert the idea, thought lost since the Kansas-Nebraska Act, that freedom was the default setting and slavery only ever the exception. In time, the United States would become either a slave nation or a free-labour nation: a house divided against itself, he warned in a famous metaphor, could not stand.

Historians are as guilty as the wider public in their generally rosy assessment of Lincoln. Few other historical figures are still treated with such a curious mix of familiarity, reverence, admiration, affection and solemnity. But, even so, historians disagree about the depth and consistency of his anti-slavery commitment. Some contend he was always driven by a moral anti-slavery purpose but was canny about how to advance his case in a conservative country; others that he was by nature a moderate and a compromiser, genuinely willing to see slavery continue so long as the Federal government could distance itself from culpability.

What seems most likely is that he never anticipated (and why should he?) that he would end up as the leading figure in an unimaginably destructive war. Had his new administration been able to face down secession in short order, there is no reason to believe that slavery would have ended during his administration. But once it was clear, from at least May 1862 onwards, that the United States was engaged in a far more serious and existential undertaking, slavery was always bound to be at stake, and Lincoln, with his personal hope that "all men, everywhere, could be free", felt increasingly certain that there was a providential purpose at work that was driving him and those around him towards a final settlement of the issue that had scarred and divided the Republic since the outset.

Why did the South secede?

Strictly speaking, the "South" as a whole never did. This question should really be: why did individual slaveholding states secede, beginning with South Carolina in the weeks immediately following Lincoln's election? Four slave states (Delaware, Kentucky, Maryland and Missouri) never seceded at all, while four others (North Carolina, Arkansas, Tennessee and Virginia) only did so after President Lincoln had called for troops to put down the rebellion. The seceding states published formal justifications or their leaders made public pronouncements declaring that their motivation was protecting slavery.

South Carolina secessionists, for example, denounced the free states for attacking "as sinful the institution of Slavery", allowing abolitionist societies to be formed, trying to prevent slaveholders from taking their "property" into the western territories, and inciting slaves to run away and rebel. Notwithstanding the claims of present-day neo-Confederate apologists, South Carolina and the rest did not leave the Union over an abstract point of constitutional principle ("states' rights"), nor because of disagreements over the level at which tariffs should be set (though there *were* such disagreements).

By 9th February 1861, commissioners from the seven seceded states, meeting in Montgomery, Alabama, had adopted a provisional Constitution and Jefferson Davis of Mississippi became the provisional president of the Confederate States of America. Even so, the tide of secession was held back by Unionists in the Upper South states of North Carolina, Tennessee and Arkansas. And in Virginia, still the state with the largest number of slaves, secession was opposed by a majority of the slave-owning political elite, who argued that the Union, notwithstanding the election of a "Black Republican" president, still provided more security for slavery than an untested Southern Confederacy. Conscious that Lincoln's election had been entirely legitimate, some urged that the South wait for an "overt act" of aggression by the new administration. That "overt act" soon came, however, as we will see, and by May 1861 eleven slave states had formed the Confederacy and were prepared to defend their independence.

It is astonishing, in retrospect, that secession took Northerners by surprise, but it did. They had, after all, had plenty of notice: Southerners had been warning for years of disunion. But even when secession ordinances were passed by the first seven "deep South" states, and even after an alternative confederation was formed, many Northerners (including the president-elect, Abraham Lincoln) continued to behave as if this was all a great bluff and that the "latent" Unionism of the Southern people would come to the fore.

There was an orchestrated political plan by a group of secessionists to seize the moment after

Lincoln's election. In that sense, Northerners were right to think, as they did, that secession was a top-down process. In most cases, however, secession was also endorsed by popular ballots. Even those who were reluctant accepted it when it had happened: their loyalty to their state trumped loyalty to the Union. For ordinary Southerners, this was about honour – maintaining their dignity in the face of what they saw as the indignity of an extremist movement (the "Black Republican Party"), which threatened, by its very existence, to stir up slave revolts. Then to be told by the new president that they had no right to leave the Union, and that they were rebels and would be invaded, solidified the pro-secessionist ranks as nothing else could have done.

JEFFERSON DAVIS

Jefferson Davis seemed an impressive choice as provisional president (and then the only officially elected president) of the Confederate States of America. With his tall, distinguished bearing he looked the part. He had served as US Secretary of War in the early 1850s, and was a graduate of the West Point military academy. He was born, like Lincoln, in Kentucky, but the Davises, already more prosperous than the Lincolns, moved South instead of North to further their family's fortunes and Jefferson grew up on his brother's cotton plantation in Mississippi. He remained, to the end of his life, a powerful defender of slavery.

Davis's military experience may, in the end, however, have been as much of a burden as an advantage in his unhappy time as the civilian leader of the Confederacy. In contrast to his

The new Confederate constitution mimicked the old United States Constitution in almost every respect. If this now seems ironic, it did not to Confederates who saw themselves as the continuation of the original intention of the (mainly Southern) Founding Fathers. It was, they thought, the North that had subverted the original intention of the Republic. "*We* are not revolutionists," protested the influential Southern editor J. D. B. De Bow. Indeed, agreed the "fire-eater", Robert Barnwell Rhett, it was the "Black Republicans" who were the "the practical revolutionists and hatchers of trouble".*

One of the ways in which the Confederate

* Quoted in Sean Wilentz, *The Rise of American Democracy: Jefferson to Lincoln* (New York: Norton, 2005), p. 773.

nemesis in the White House, he was seemingly incapable of delegating responsibility and interfered incessantly in the minuscule details of military planning. Weighed down by various illnesses, he gained a reputation as cold and humourless. When he disagreed with people, he seemed incapable of not turning it into a personal squabble. Feuds within his cabinet, with members of the Confederate Congress and with State Governors undermined his authority. And – again in contrast to Lincoln –

he lacked the knack of being able to articulate his cause with clarity and conviction.

The unflattering comparison with Lincoln has been Davis's undoing among historians. One notable scholar even went so far as to suggest that had their roles been reversed, the outcome of the war would have been different.

As so often in thinking about history, it is almost impossible not to be influenced by hindsight: Davis, unlike Lincoln, was a loser; his cause not only failed on the battlefield

Constitution did depart from the Federal version was revealing. It directly invoked "the favor and guidance of Almighty God". Southern clergy, who had long provided a Biblical justification for slavery, reassured Southerners that theirs was a truly Christian nation, engaged in a holy war against infidel invaders. Southerners would prevail, the new president, Jefferson Davis, explained, because they maintained a "firm reliance on that Divine Power which covers with its protection the just cause, and we will continue to struggle for our inherent right to freedom, independence, and self-government".[*] Even when the South lost battles, clergymen warned that God was testing the resilience of the nation through the

***

*   Quoted in Rable, *Confederate Republic*, p. 75.

***

but has been castigated by posterity as morally wrong. In truth, he was an intelligent, if reserved man, who had a near-impossible job. Had the Confederacy been able to capitalise on its early military successes and had internal weaknesses in the Union led to peace negotiations – as seemed possible even as late as the summer of 1864 – Davis's historical reputation would no doubt be very different.

After the end of the war, Jefferson Davis was briefly imprisoned but never brought to trial. He long outlived most of his enemies in the North as well as his rivals in the South, dying in 1889 at the venerable age of 81. By that time, he had, inevitably, written his memoirs, an unrepentant defence of the rebellion as a principled resistance to centralised government.

Although he never renounced his defence of slavery, his post-war career did much to lay the foundation for the myth that what motivated the South was the abstract notion of "states' rights". ∎

trial of war. Redemption lay through further sacrifice.

Why did the North respond to secession with a war to save the Union?

Between the Revolution and the Civil War there were two competing views of the nature of the American Union. One, championed by Southerners, was that it was a contract between sovereign states, freely entered into and therefore soluble at any time. The other was that the Constitution had formed a perpetual Union, constituted by the people directly not by the states.

This second view was the one that was widely accepted in the North in the antebellum period. Advocates of the idea of perpetual union pointed out that the Constitution had been ratified by the people of the original 13 states, and that, in any case, most of the states in the Union (by 1860 there were 19 free states and 14 slave states) had come into it only *after* the ratification of the Constitution. Having no prior existence they could hardly be said to have freely entered the United States. (The possible exceptions to this were Louisiana and Texas, which had existed prior to American annexation from France and Mexico respectively).

This was the legal reasoning that led opponents of secession to regard it as illegitimate. Abraham Lincoln never acknowledged in any public speech or document that the seceded states had left the Union: he referred to "combinations" that were "impeding" the execution of the laws of the United States, and to "rebels"; but he made no mention of such a thing as the Confederacy and refused to legitimise his formidable military opponents as being authorised by a state. From the point of view of the United States, the war was merely a police operation on a massive scale.

But this constitutional rationale tells us only part of the story of why massive state violence was regarded as a necessary response to the creation of a breakaway Confederacy.

Northerners had come to believe that the Union was much more than simply their form of government; it was as they saw it, in the vanguard of human progress. To break it up was treason. Even more than that, it was a betrayal of the future of the human race, the hope of liberty and self-government. At Gettysburg in November 1863, in the 200-word speech that has become his most famous, Lincoln summarised the Union cause as the battle to determine whether government "of the people, for the people, by the people" would "perish from the earth". This was the idea of American exceptionalism – the notion that the US had a uniquely redemptive role in world history, an idea with roots in the first Puritan settlers in New

England. The first governor of the Massachusetts Bay Colony, John Winthrop, had given a sermon, famous ever since, in which he talked about his errand into the wilderness as like creating a "city upon a hill, the eyes of the world upon us". If those were the stakes it is no wonder that Northerners were prepared to suffer the extraordinary sacrifices they did to hold the Union together.

For Northerners, the notion that the Union might continue after secession, albeit in truncated form, seemed inconceivable. There was an element of geographical determinism here – a deep-seated sense that the United States was providentially destined to dominate the North American continent. If two rival nations emerged, the New World, it was feared, would become like the old: a squabbling mess of petty principalities instead of the "Empire of Liberty" envisaged by Thomas Jefferson. Americans would find themselves rapidly subjected to tariff barriers, taxes for armies, and borders impeding opportunities to move West and settle on "virgin" land. Secession, then, could only be seen as an attempt to destroy the Union.

The principle of secession, was furthermore, Northerners argued, a direct challenge to the ideal of free government not just because it broke up the "last best hope of earth" but also because it was a rejection by a minority of majority rule. By seceding as a direct response to a presidential election result they didn't like, and then (in the case of the Upper

South states) by seceding because they were not prepared to participate in the effort to enforce the laws, the rebels were challenging the core idea of democracy. Secession, Lincoln insisted in his inaugural address, was "the essence of anarchy". It could be dressed up in quasi-legal forms, but it was the same basic idea: a wilful rejection of duly constituted authority. In this sense, the Northern war effort had nothing to do with slavery. It was, instead, a fundamentally conservative effort to preserve not just the territorial integrity of the United States but also law and order.

This underlying preservationist narrative was reinforced by the manner in which the war began. The first shots were fired at 4.30am on 12th April 1861 by South Carolina forces. Their target was Fort Sumter, an island in Charleston harbour garrisoned by US troops. The new president, Abraham Lincoln had, perhaps deliberately, precipitated this aggression by making public his plan to re-supply (though not reinforce) the fort.

By opening fire on Fort Sumter, the Confederates played into Lincoln's hands, making the issue a test of whether a free government could defend itself. The image of the stars and stripes under fire rallied the North in defence of the Union, overshadowing the slavery issue entirely. Newspapers, which the day before had argued for compromise and a cooling of passions, now called for vengeance and urged their readers to rally behind the flag. On 15 April Lincoln summoned

75,000 volunteers under the 1792 Militia Act to serve for 90 days, the maximum amount prescribed by the law. This was the "overt act" of "aggression" that prompted the states of Virginia, North Carolina, Arkansas and Tennessee to join their fellow Southern slave states in seceding.

Strictly speaking, then, the North did not wage war in response to secession per se, but in response to a specific act – the firing on a US fort. The rebels, literally as well as figuratively, fired on the American flag. That triggered talk of dishonour and Northern "manhood" being challenged. How, given the deep wells of nationalist feeling, could Northerners fail to respond to such an outrage?

One further reason explains Northern willingness to go to war in April 1861: they wanted war for its own sake. This may seem a bold claim. And of course no one in April 1861 knew that the conflict that was being launched would last for four bloody years. When people imagined war, they imagined a rapid, heroic fight with the outcome determined by the valour of the combatants. There was a strong feeling that confrontation would be cathartic and salutary.

What was the military strategy of each side?

At first, both sides hoped and expected that the war would be over in one grand battle. Men rushed to join up for fear of missing all the action. Only a minority predicted the long and brutal struggle that ensued. After a phoney war of several weeks, with small skirmishes between hastily formed armies, a big battle did take place just outside Washington D.C., at a small creek called Bull Run. The cavalry on both sides operated seemingly at random, certainly without any proper co-ordination with infantry attacks. Troops mistook units on their own side for the enemy, and on several occasions opened fire. After an inconclusive few hours, the Union army was sent into panic-stricken retreat by a Confederate attack. The casualty figures in this first great conflict were tiny compared to the carnage of later battles, yet at the time, the deaths of 1,982 Confederates and 2,896 Federal soldiers shocked both sides profoundly.

While Southerners rejoiced at their victory, Northerners were forced to confront for the first time the scale of the undertaking they had so blithely embraced. All the one-day battle clarified was that this would be a longer struggle.

The public and politicians had come to understand that the confrontation would not be resolved without a sustained war effort. So how should the North try to win? By occupying territory? Targeting rebel forces? Or trying to capture the Southern capital city (Richmond, Virginia, just 90 miles south of Washington)? Should the Confederacy be surrounded by a cordon and strangled to death, or should Northern armies march into the heart of Dixie? Northern strategy combined, messily and inconsistently, all of these approaches.

The Union's advantages were clear. It had more than twice the population (when the South's

THE BATTLE OF GETTYSBURG

Gettysburg, a small college town in Pennsylvania, was where the Union army finally caught up with Lee's Confederates, who had audaciously invaded this free state in an effort to bring the war to the Northern people.

Over three days, from 1st to 3rd July 1863, Union and Confederate troops fought the battle that has since been mythologised as the pivotal moment of the war. The culmination, on the third day, was when Lee ordered three divisions led by General George E. Pickett to attack the Federal centre. It was a bloody, much-memorialised disaster.

All 13 colonels in Pickett's division were killed or wounded. Fewer than half of the Confederate attackers made it back to their lines. In total, Lee lost a third of his men in the three days and his army never fully recovered. The battle, in many ways, marked high water for the South. Although it was nearly two years from Lee's retreat to the final surrender at Appomattox, never again did Confederate forces present the same kind of military challenge. ∎

enslaved population was discounted), and almost all the nation's industrial capacity. It had a much better rail network, making the movement of troops and supplies much easier. With access to foreign currency, it was still able to export goods. And with a growing workforce, resupplied by continuing immigration, it was better able to shoulder the immense cost of war through taxes and loans. All of these advantages led some foreign observers to conclude that the North could not fail; or, at least, couldn't fail so long as these advantages

THE GETTYSBURG ADDRESS

The most famous of Lincoln's speeches was a two-minute address to dedicate the military cemetery at Gettysburg on 19th November 1863. Lincoln was not the main speaker; he only wound up proceedings; but it is his words that are remembered. "Four score and seven years ago," he began, "our fathers brought forth on this continent a new nation, conceived in liberty and dedicated to the proposition that all men are created equal." The effect of this opening sentence was to date the origins of the republic to the Declaration of Independence of 1776, with its grand preamble authored by Jefferson and appealing to the universal ideal of equality – rather than to the more work-manlike Federal Constitution of 1787. Lincoln was implying that the Constitution merely gave form to the nation, and that the nation mattered not as an end in itself but as an embodiment of the idea of equality and liberty.

Echoing in secular language the Christian idea of a trial of faith, Lincoln went on to claim that the Civil War was a test of

were brought to bear. The surprising – and, for the North, frustrating – aspect of the first two years of the war was that these advantages were invisible. More often than not the Union had more troops than the Confederacy in battles, but the difference was seldom decisive.

If the North didn't know how to use its greater manpower, nor was it always clear what Union armies were trying to achieve. Newspapers pressured the government with cries of "On to Richmond!" on the assumption that taking out the

"whether that nation or any nation so conceived and so dedicated can long endure". In little more than 200 words, he explained why the struggle and the sacrifice had a dignity and a purpose of universal and transcendent significance: "that this nation under God shall have a new birth of freedom, and that government of the people, by the people, for the people shall not perish from the earth".

The historian Gary Wills wrote a very influential book in the 1990s claiming that the Gettysburg Address had "remade" America by placing the ideals of freedom and equality at its heart. Although Lincoln's words were praised at the time, no one seemed to think that his ideas were new. As so often with Lincoln's speeches, he simply articulated with beautiful elegance what others were saying in more cumbersome ways.

And we should not misread one of his most resonant phrases, "a new birth of freedom": although modern historians often assume this was an allusion to the end of slavery, Lincoln's listeners understood him to be meaning freedom in a much broader sense – the liberation (for white Americans) that would come with the restoration of the Union with its transcendent purpose of spreading liberty. The destruction of slavery was clearly a means to that end, but it was not the end in itself. ∎

Confederate capital would end the war. Huge resources were expended trying to achieve this goal, with the result that the main focus of the public's attention was on the campaigns fought in northern Virginia. Yet the Union army's repeated failures in Virginia reinforced Confederate morale, while the more serious blows to the Confederacy's capacity were struck in the west, where, with less press attention, Union armies gradually gained control of first the upper reaches of the Mississippi River and then, with a naval assault in the spring of 1862, of the great river's mouth at New Orleans. Eventually, by the summer of 1863, the whole of the river, running north to south, was in Union hands, cutting the Confederacy in two.

While armies clashed in the woods of Virginia, more progress was also made by a less dramatic strategy of taking and holding key enclaves in the South, from which raids into rebel territory could be launched. Usually these were strongholds taken from the sea, such as the South Carolina Sea Islands. Although the Confederacy achieved the extraordinary feat of building an iron-clad warship that duelled to a draw with a Union iron-clad ship, the naval advantage always lay with the United States, giving them the opportunity to attack the South's long and essentially indefensible coastline.

For the most part, the armies of both sections were improvised. There was a United States army in 1861 but it was tiny, largely officered by Southerners who resigned their commissions as their states seceded, and much of it was posted in the west, conducting warfare against Native Americans. The Civil War armies were made up overwhelmingly of volunteers. Initially, Lincoln's call for troops mobilised the state militias, a long-established institution of volunteers intended to defend public order. Militias were regarded as a republican alternative to the autocratic institution of standing armies. The first volunteers signed up for three months only, and at the end of their terms, some returned home. The next tranche of volunteers were enlisted for three years – that is, until the autumn of 1864 – which was presumed to be quite long enough to defeat a rag-tag rebel insurgency.

In fact, the rebels proved capable of mounting highly successful military campaigns. Young men in the seceded states clamoured to join up when the war commenced. Southerners were convinced that they could "whip" the Yankees easily; how could a pale-faced mechanic fight as well as a Southern farm boy, especially when the Southerner was fighting for his home and hearth against invasion?

But if the Confederacy's objective – independence – was clear, its means of accomplishing it was less so. A defensive war might suggest a strategy of falling back, like the Russians in the face of Napoleon, and staging devastating counter-attacks to cut the enemy's supply lines. In the end Southern armies did exactly this, but their original hope was very different. They wanted to win a defensive war by going on the offensive.

In the first two years, Confederate armies adopted a highly aggressive approach to battles. Inspired by the boldness of Napoleon, Southern commanders divided their forces in the face of the enemy and launched daring and unexpected assaults. Quite often, especially when the troops were led, as they were from May 1862 onwards in Virginia, by the charismatic General Robert E. Lee, this offensive approach paid dividends. Lee's outnumbered army rebuffed the cumbersome manouevres of the grippingly cautious Union general George McClellan in a series of brilliant victories during the so-called Seven Days' Battles, ending in the space of a week the North's confident expectation that Richmond would fall and the war would be over by the summer of 1862.

Not content with pushing Union troops away from the Confederate capital, Lee then astonished his adversaries even more by marching his army into Maryland – one of the four Border slave states that remained in the Union. The following summer, 1863, he invaded Pennsylvania, a free state. Once there, the army plundered the countryside and rounded up free-born blacks, to be marched south into slavery "just like we drive cattle", as one appalled Chambersburg woman expressed it.[*]

The offensive tactics of the Confederate army

[*]   James C. Mohr, *The Cormany Diaries: A Northern Family in the Civil War* (Pittsburgh: University of Pennsylvania Press, 1982), p. 330.

were a necessity, despite their overall defensive posture, because Southern public opinion demanded it. Having made the choice that slavery would be better preserved in a new Confederacy than in the Union, the core aim of the rebel government had to be to hold and secure its territory; tactical retreats would have undermined its very raison d'être. And only by taking war on to Northern soil could they make Northerners behind the lines feel the cost of war – and only then could pressure be brought to bear that might lead the North to call off its attempt at military subjugation.

Nothing the Confederacy could do, however, prevented the war from being fought, overwhelmingly, on Southern soil, and the most consequential battles were fought in the east, in the northern part of Virginia between Washington and Richmond. While recognising, to a greater or lesser extent, the importance of controlling strategic rail and water routes and of destroying Confederate forces, and the advantages of occupying territory, the Lincoln administration and the military leadership remained fixated on the Confederate capital. Equally, the symbolism of Richmond meant that the South could not evacuate the city until they had to, just days before the de facto end of the war.

TEN FACTS ABOUT
THE AMERICAN CIVIL WAR

1.
About a third of the men who fought in the Civil War were immigrants, with those from Great Britain forming by the far the largest single group, followed by Germans and Irish.

2.
Generals were 50% more likely to die in the Civil War than privates, owing to their determination to lead, in many cases literally, from the front.

3.
The Civil War helped to popularise photography, through the portraits of newly volunteered loved ones in uniform and through the post-battle photographs showing dead bodies and horses that caused huge a sensation when they were displayed in New York City in 1862.

4.
More men died from disease than from battle wounds, with most deaths due to diarrhoea.

5.
The last documented Civil War veteran, Albert Henry Woolson, died in 1956 at the age of 109.

6.
General Ambrose E. Burnside, who briefly commanded the Union Army of the Potomac and led it to one its worst disasters at Fredericksburg, gave his name to the term "burnsides" to describe a then-popular arrangement of facial hair.

7.
It is estimated that around 400 women disguised themselves as men to fight in the Civil War.

8.
Nathan Bedford Forrest, who was one of the leaders of the Ku Klux Klan after the war, had 29 horses shot from under him.

9.
There was a Union general called Jefferson Davis, bearing the same name as the President of the Confederacy.

10.
"Stonewall" Jackson, the legendary Confederate general, was a major hypochondriac. He rode with his left arm raised because he thought it helped his blood to flow better and never ate pepper because he thought it made his left leg weak.

What was the European reaction to the outbreak of war?

The dog that didn't bark in the American Civil War was foreign intervention. The Confederacy had placed great hopes on the European powers coming to their aid. Just as the French military intervention on behalf of the rebel colonists had defeated the British at Yorktown in 1781, Confederates fantasised about a British military force helping them tip the balance against the Yankees. Apart from any ideological considerations, Confederates believed they held a trump card: "King Cotton". Nearly 90% of raw cotton imports into the United Kingdom in 1859 came from the Southern states. And this cotton was the great fuel of the British industrial economy.

There were certainly conservative British politicians who were deeply sympathetic to the Confederacy, partly through a sense of *schadenfreude* at the collapse of the upstart American democracy, and partly through a feeling that Southerners shared more similar, aristocratic values than the materialistic Yankees. Then there were liberals, including the Chancellor of the Exchequer, William Gladstone, who saw the Confederates attempting to create a nation in much the same way as the Italians or Hungarians were.

In an age of liberal nationalism, perhaps liberal sympathies should be with a nascent nation struggling to come into existence against the attempt by a quasi-imperial power in Washington to subdue it?

So why did the British not intervene – at least to the extent of recognising the Confederacy diplomatically, even if not sending actual military aid?

Part of the answer is that the Confederacy did not play cotton diplomacy very well. Rather than using their cotton exports to secure much-needed European loans, the Richmond government initially tried to institute a cotton embargo. They burned bales of raw cotton waiting on the dockside at New Orleans to be exported to Liverpool, in the hope that cotton-reliant Britain would then be forced to give them aid. This crude blackmail went down badly in Whitehall. The South also misjudged the timing of the impact: cotton stockpiles by textile manufacturers meant that it wasn't until the second half of 1862 that the mills of Lancashire, Yorkshire and Lanarkshire started feeling the shortage. When they did, the effect was dramatic, with unemployment or short hours affecting 80% of workers in some mill towns. But by then the balance of risk for the British in intervening had shifted.

The Emancipation Proclamation changed the terms of debate. Now it was harder to present the Union cause as analogous to the Austrian repression of Italy's aspirations to nationhood; now, the war in North America more clearly held the future of the world's most powerful and wealthy slaveholders in the balance. As an abolitionist power, Britain would have found it nearly impossible to side with the slaveholding South.

The closest Britain came to military involvement was over shipping rights. The US navy tried to seize – and, on occasion, succeeded in seizing – British merchant vessels bound for neutral ports near the Confederate coast such as the Bahamas or Cuba, on the grounds that the cargo was then to be transferred to Southern blockade-runners. Britain had done much the

ROBERT E. LEE

Robert E. Lee was born into an aristocratic Virginian family fallen on straightened times (his father, a former Governor, ended up in briefly in a debtors' prison). Lee nevertheless attended expensive schools, funded by his wealthier relations, and excelled at the West Point military academy. Before the Civil War, he had a career in the US army, fighting in the Mexican War, and, as a colonel, commanding the forces that captured the abolitionist John Brown at Harpers Ferry.

Lee's views on slavery were fairly liberal by the standards of his class and region. In 1856, in a letter to his wife, he referred to slavery as a "moral & political evil in any Country". He went to on to say, however, that he thought it "a greater evil to the white man than to the black race, & while my feelings are strongly enlisted in behalf of the latter, my sympathies are more strong for the former". Back in the 1820s, the slaveholding author of the Declaration of Independence, Thomas Jefferson, had described the

same to American shipping during the Napoleonic wars, and at the time the US had protested fiercely. Now the roles were reversed.

The conflict came to a head on 8th November 1861, when sailors from the USS *San Jacinto* boarded a British ship, the *Trent*, 300 miles east of Havana and removed two Confederate envoys en route to Europe to press Britain and France for support. The British government was furious at the violation of its flag and there was talk of war. The diplomatic row was defused after the US Secretary of State apologised and released the envoys – though insisting, as he did so, that the

dilemma of slavery as being like "holding a wolf by the ears": you do not want to hold it, but you dare not let it go. By the late 1850s, Lee had seemingly come to a similar view. Furthermore, like many other Americans at the time, including Northerners, he thought that slavery served a function in "civilising" African American people. "The blacks," he wrote, "are immeasurably better off here than in Africa, morally, socially & physically. The painful discipline they are undergoing, is necessary for their instruction as a race, & I hope will prepare & lead them to better things.'"

Lee was seen by the builders of the "Lost Cause" narrative as the exemplar of the nobility of the Southern way of life so brutally destroyed by materialistic Yankee invaders. The war, in this telling, was not about slavery, and the claim that Lee himself was anti-slavery was a vital component of this myth.

It was also claimed – again with some plausibility – that Lee opposed secession and supported his state's military effort only reluctantly. He did not, however, oppose secession on principle. His political outlook was that of a temperamental conservative: pessimistic about human perfectibility and sceptical about

case proved that the British had finally accepted the United States's conception of neutral shipping rights.

The pressure for war over the *Trent* affair was real, but Britain, like France, would have had more to lose than to gain by diplomatic recognition of the Confederacy, with the corollary of war with the United States. Huge European financial investment in the US, not least in the railroads that had been built in the 1850s, meant that bankers had solid reasons to oppose war. Perhaps, had it looked likely that the Confederacy was going to win, self-interest might have pushed Britain and France to come in

revolutionary and utopian schemes. The Confederacy, he wrote to his son in 1861, was a "revolution" that betrayed the Founding Fathers. "I can anticipate no greater calamity for the country," Lee wrote, "than a dissolution of the Union."

After Lincoln called for troops to put down the rebellion, Lee was offered command of Union forces. He was torn, but his loyalty to Virginia trumped his loyalty to the Union. "I look upon secession as anarchy. If I owned the four millions of slaves in the South I would sacrifice them all to the Union; but how can I draw my sword upon Virginia, my native state?"

In the first year of the war, Lee was a military advisor to the new Confederate President Jefferson Davis, but his ascent to the status of almost a demi-god came the following spring when he took command of the Confederate Army of Northern Virginia and triumphed in the Seven Days' Battles. For the following year, until the battle of Gettysburg in July 1863, he appeared invincible. He won a series of stunning victories, outsmarting his enemies at the Second Battle of Bull Run and at Chancellorsville.

With a sombre mien and courtly deportment, his elegant

belatedly on their side, but they had no interest in backing a loser. Far from being the decisive external factor that would win it for the South, foreign intervention would only ever have likely been a consequence, not a cause, of Confederate military victory.

For millions of people in Europe, the United States had long been a beacon of freedom. Newspapers, especially in Britain, but also in Germany, reprinted letters from emigrants to America reporting on the struggle for liberty. This did not feel, to many ordinary Europeans, like a foreign war so much as a struggle that touched the

---

grey uniform and tall white horse, Traveller, his apparently unflappable leadership and his quiet determination, Lee quickly came to embody the Confederate cause, far eclipsing Jefferson Davis. To a deeply religious white Southern population he was the ultimate Christian warrior, and so, when the tide of war began to turn, his fate became the touchstone for the success of the revolution.

The surrender at Appomattox was, in some ways, his finest hour. His dignity in defeat and his final order to his men to go home peacefully and be good citizens of the United States solidified his claim to have

not only fought bravely but to have laid the basis for a peaceful reunion that, in the "Lost Cause" myth, was destroyed only by the zealotry of vengeful Northern radicals. Lee was never arrested or imprisoned. He settled into a distinguished retirement as president of Washington and Lee University, and after his death in 1870 his reputation soared. By the end of the 19th century, even Northerners seemed to revere him as a great American, an ironic position from which he has never quite been dislodged. ∎

* Quoted in Douglas S. Freeman, *R. E. Lee: A Biography* (New York: Scribner's, 1934), p. 372.

same basic question that they contended for at home: the power of "the people" against entrenched, aristocratic interests. The overlapping question of slavery played into this perception. The Union, especially after 1862, represented not just the hope of democratic change for everyone, but also the last great battle against slavery.

How and why did emancipation come to be an objective of the North?

This is possibly the question that divides Civil War historians more than any other. For many years the assumption was that the war began as a crusade to save the Union but along the way became a war for a grander and more morally uplifting end: emancipation. It is a powerful narrative that makes sense of a lot of what happened in the war.

In July 1861, Congress passed a series of resolutions emphatically declaring that the Union – and only the Union – was the objective of the war. Even Republicans who were unabashed in their dislike of slavery went out of their way to emphasise that the war had national restoration as its simple objective. Yet by the summer of 1862, Congress was authorising the army to emancipate slaves. This was reinforced by the president's two emancipation proclamations on 22nd September 1862 and on 1st January 1863. Later that year, black troops, including tens of thousands of former slaves, were fighting for the Union (albeit on lower pay and in segregated units). This seemed the ultimate evidence that the war had changed its purpose.

But was this not so much a shift in the purpose of the war as the unfolding of an anti-slavery agenda that was there from the start? Although Republicans like Lincoln always denied that they had any intention to interfere with slavery where it existed (they had no choice, after all, given the Federal structure of the republic), there were many precedents in the past for military eman-cipation.

Certainly there were plenty of African Americans and abolitionists who assumed that the firing of the first shot of the war signalled the end of slavery. A very conservative Philadelphian, Sidney George Fisher, recorded in his diary at the start of 1861 that "the moral feeling of the North is setting strongly against slavery & the southern politicians [by their unreasonable demands and now their attempt to destroy the Union] are the cause of it". And when the war began, the biggest circulation newspaper in the country, the *New York Tribune,* described the conflict as the "Slaveholders' Rebellion". Logically, if it was the slaveholders who were in rebellion, it was not so much of a leap to get to the view that by destroying slavery the rebellion would be destroyed too. An 1861 editorial set out what the newspaper saw as the underlying conflict in the war: "the idea of slavery is fighting the idea of freedom".

Other Northerners, though, did not think this way. They accepted that the war was caused by slavery, but they could also have lived with a restoration of the Union that left slavery in place. For them, union was indeed the sole objective. And some historians have argued that that always remained the case. Even Lincoln, it is suggested, embraced his emancipation policy only reluctantly as a *tool* with which to subdue the rebellion and never as an end in itself. Whatever the intentions of Northerners, or their inner motives when taking up arms, they were all too aware that the situation in which they found themselves was fast moving.

From the very start, the Union army had to make decisions about whether to encourage the dismantling of slavery. Wherever there was a Union military presence in a slave state, enslaved people sought sanctuary. Some Union generals sent them back to their owners, others – the ones with anti-slavery leanings – allowed them to stay. Refugee camps grew up around military camps.

It was General Benjamin Butler, in command of a Union-held enclave in Virginia, who found a way of protecting runaway slaves without publicly challenging the official line that the Union did not seek emancipation. In the summer of 1861, he announced that any fugitive slave who sought refuge with his forces would be held as "contraband of war". This phrase deftly turned against the South arguments that slaves were property. Just as horses or artillery, if captured, could legitimately be impounded since they were likely to be of military value to the enemy, so too "human property", likely to be used to dig fortifications or supply the Confederate army, could be "seized" – and effectively freed. For the rest of the war, "contraband" became the normal term to describe refugees who were formerly enslaved.

The role of the army as a de facto army of liberation was formalised by an Act of Congress passed in July 1862, innocuously entitled the Confiscation Act. It required Union commanders – whatever their private political beliefs – to emancipate slaves with whom they came into contact and therefore not to respect Southern slave laws or the Federal Fugitive Slave Act (although that remained on the statue books and loyal slaveholders in the Border states still attempted to use it).

There remained powerful opposition to the emancipation policy from within the army, but the majority seemed to accept it. There is also evidence that the reality of confronting enslaved people, often for the first time, shifted the attitudes of some. Union soldiers who had grown up in anti-slavery households interpreted their encounters with freed slaves in the light of what they had heard of the cruelties of slavery. Private Chauncey Cooke wrote to his mother in Wisconsin about "a toothless old slave with one blind eye" who told him horrific stories of his wife and children having been sold, of whippings and being hunted by bloodhounds when he tried to escape. The stories, Cooke wrote his mother, were "just like the ones in Uncle Tom's Cabin and I believe them".* Some Union troops were convinced by evangelical preachers and anti-slavery propaganda that expunging the sin of slavery would redeem their country. Some simply wanted black troops to be placed in the front line instead of them. Most were probably convinced by the much more pragmatic case that if the rebels hated emancipation, then it must be a good thing. Emancipation was a weapon which, whatever its merits on its own terms, struck at the heart of Southern society.

Finally, the Emancipation Proclamation of 22nd September 1862 warned rebel states that if they did not return to the Union by 1st January, their slaves would be regarded as free. Jefferson Davis called this "the most execrable measure in the history of guilty man". The three-month delay was meant to send a clear message that emancipation was a tool of war rather than an end in itself. On 1st January Lincoln duly issued the Emancipation Proclamation. It applied only to those areas of the United States still in arms against the government. Lincoln took a political and strategic risk in coupling the fate of the Union

* Chauncey Herbert Cooke, March 20, 1863, in *Soldier Boy's Letters to His Father and Mother*, 1861-1865 (n.p., 1915), p. 28.

with the fate of slavery. In some Union regiments there were near-mutinies at the news. But abolitionists rejoiced that at last the day of Jubilee was at hand.

To declare slaves free when they were under the control of the Confederate government was not, in practice, to free them (though several thousand slaves were directly liberated on 1st January as a result of the Proclamation). In practice, what the Emancipation Proclamation did was to give further weight to Congress's decision that Union troops should free slaves when they came into contact with them. The problem for slaves, though, was that the war touched too few of them. The Confederate states covered an area larger than Western Europe. Only a tiny fraction was ever occupied by Union forces. According to one estimate 90% of the enslaved population was still enslaved when the war came to an end.

This reminds us that *emancipation* and *abolition* are different processes. The former relates to the freeing of individuals; the latter to changing laws to eliminate the institution altogether. The Union army emancipated some slaves (or rather, the army enabled the slaves to emancipate themselves), but abolition would require something else. That something was the Thirteenth Amendment to the Constitution, which was passed by Congress in January 1865 and ratified by the requisite number of states in December of that year. Only then, many months after the Confederacy had collapsed, did abolition happen, because only then were state laws enforcing slavery rendered unconstitutional.

For the vast majority of Northerners, the moral purpose of upholding the Union always trumped the moral purpose of emancipation. But for a majority, the former came to encompass the latter. And while there were some Northerners whose opposition to emancipation rested on a genuine conviction that slavery was morally right, most of those who hated the emancipation policy did so because they thought it was undermining the overarching aim of Union.

As the war continued, increasing numbers of Northerners came to believe that God's purpose in creating such suffering must be a punishment for the sin of slavery. In the great abolitionist anthem,

HARRIET TUBMAN AND THE "UNDERGROUND RAILROAD"

Born into slavery in Maryland, whipped and beaten as a child, Harriet Tubman escaped to Philadelphia in 1849 and then became active in the "Underground Railroad".

Repeatedly returning secretly into the slave state of Maryland, she aided the rescue of her family and other enslaved people, helping them to the relative safety of free states like Pennsylvania –and in some cases, ultimately, to the security of Canada.

Later christened "Moses" for her dangerous work, Tubman had an uncanny ability to travel undetected in slave territory, which also made her a valuable asset to the Union military when war broke out.

"The Battle Hymn of the Republic", Christ is seen in the "watch-fires of a hundred circling camps" and in the "burnished rows of steel" of the soldiers' bayonets. The Union army was the army of the Lord. In his second inaugural address, Lincoln abjured any triumphalism and instead spoke of "this terrible war" as judgment on both North and South for the offence of American slavery. Perhaps, he speculated, only when "every drop of blood drawn with the lash shall be paid by another drawn with the sword" would the war end.

Like other abolitionists, she was convinced that a war against slaveholders would lead, in the end, to abolition. She took matters into her own hands, leading expeditions behind enemy lines in South Carolina, reporting on military installations and helping slaves to escape to Union lines. In the most dramatic episode in her eventful war, she helped guide a fleet of Union steamers past Confederate mines on the Combahee River in South Carolina. Union troops burned plantations and seized property, and the sound of the steamboats' whistles attracted more than 750 slaves, who piled onto the steamboats to escape.

But Tubman's war service was never properly recognised. She received no regular pay and only in her later years, especially after the publication of her biography in the 1880s (and before her death in 1913), did she become known even within the black community. ■

Did the character of the war change?

The character of the war evolved rather than transformed suddenly, but there is no doubt that it was different in 1864 from three years earlier. Some historians have described the shift as being towards "total war", a term first used to describe the conditions of all-out warfare in the global conflicts of the 20th century. This has two related dimensions: a claim about the extent to which civilians were drawn into the military experience, and a claim about the unrestrained character of military strategy and tactics.

Whether the Civil War became a "total war" depends, of course, on how exactly you define the term, but it did not engage the Northern population or economy on so complete a scale as it did the South. The North remained largely untouched directly by fighting, and large segments of the economy remained geared to non-military production. Immigration continued apace into its cities, exports of agricultural produce to Europe increased in volume, and – as a marker of the ability of even young men to avoid military service at least for a while – the Harvard-Yale boat race continued throughout the war. In the Confederacy, however, the mobilisation of the white male population was one of the greatest of any nation in any war, and there was little in Southern life that was unaffected by the demands of war.

The policy of military emancipation, from scattered experiments in 1861 through to the uniform policy after the Emancipation Proclamation of 1 January 1863, was a major driver of the changing character of warfare. It effaced an important distinction between "military" and "civilian" targets in the South, since the most valuable form of southern "property" was now being actively "appropriated" by the invading Union forces.

The Proclamation also paved the way for the enlistment of black troops. Some 200,000 were fighting in segregated units by the end of the war, officered by whites (usually abolitionists), and, at least at first, paid at a lower rate than their white comrades. Yet they were fighting in Union army uniform for the destruction of the Confederacy and, naturally, with it, for the destruction of slavery. So outraged were Confederate soldiers by the use of black troops that they refused to treat them in the same way as white opponents: on several occasions, surrendering black Union troops were slaughtered rather than being held as prisoners of war, and in some cases they were enslaved.

The other driver of the changing nature of warfare was the gradual recognition by Union military commanders that to reap the benefit of their superior resources they had to assail the Confederacy from multiple points simultaneously, to stretch the enemy's capacity to meet the threat;

and to push relentlessly, without regrouping and withdrawal. Early on, Union generals failed to exploit the occasional victories they won. In September 1862, Confederate forces under Lee's command marched into Maryland, one of four slave states that had not seceded. They were forced back into Virginia after a vicious confrontation at Antietam in which 3,650 men were killed and more than 17,000 wounded. But to Lincoln's immense frustration, McClellan, the Union general, having won a limited victory, refused to pursue the retreating Confederate troops, arguing that his horses and troops needed to rest. Less than a year later, after McClellan had been dismissed, a new Union commander, General George G. Meade, inflicted on Lee his first clear-cut defeat at Gettysburg – but Meade also allowed Lee's army to retreat back into Virginia.

By 1864, the assumptions underlying Union strategy were changing. One military approach, McClellan's conception of a limited war conducted according to the highest principles of Christian civilisation, had been swept away by the emancipation policy. The limits of a second approach, the occupation of territory, were also now becoming clear. Gaining and holding territory bolstered Union morale and depressed the South – the fall of Vicksburg, Atlanta, and ultimately Richmond, are the best examples. But Lincoln understood that Confederate armies, not territory, must be the ultimate target. This was the lesson

The Battle of Atlanta on 22 July 1864.

learned by Generals Grant and Sherman in the
west, where the strategy of taking territory failed
to quash the Confederates' capacity to fight. After
all, if it had taken the Union army two years
simply to take control of eastern Tennessee where
much of the population supported the Union, how
long would it take to subdue Georgia or South
Carolina? Only the defeat of armies – Lee's Army
of Northern Virginia, above all – would mark the
war's end.

The shift to a more aggressive, all-out approach
was signalled by the appointment of Ulysses Grant
as the new Union commander in the much-watched
Virginia theatre of war in early 1864. Together

with William Sherman, commander of the Union forces fighting their way through Tennessee and into Georgia, Grant ordered a spring campaign that involved fighting continuously. This was in sharp contrast to the previous practice of great set-piece battles followed by long periods of quiet.

Grant was a stocky, hard-drinking westerner who had struggled with business failure and alcoholism before the war, but had come into his own as a pugnacious commander. While the overall strategy of Union forces was to deprive the South of the will and the capacity to continue fighting, in Virginia, as Lincoln realised, the only target that mattered was Lee's army. "Wherever the enemy goes, let our troops go also," Grant telegraphed Lincoln in August 1864. "This," replied Lincoln, "is exactly right."

Grant explained in his memoirs the evolution of his thinking about the war. The turning point for him was the Confederate counter-attack at Shiloh in 1862.

I gave up all idea of saving the Union except by complete conquest. Up to that time it had been the policy of our army... to protect the property of the citizens whose territory was invaded without regard to their sentiments, whether Union or Secession. After this, however, I regarded it as humane to both sides to protect the persons of those found at their homes, but to consume everything that could be used to support or supply armies... Their destruction was *accomplished without bloodshed, and tended to the same result as the destruction of armies. I continued this policy to the close of the war.*[*]

If, at the start of the war, Northern politicians and generals had assumed that the Union army would advance into the South in an orderly manner with little civilian resistance, such illusions had been shattered by the spring of 1862. Experience had shown that the Union army could control areas of rebel-held territory only by establishing a defensible enclave then launching a continuous war of raids. Containing such enclaves forced the Confederacy to expend valuable and often futile resources. Although it was the big battles that attracted the attention of the press and accounted for a majority of casualties, minor military encounters between raiding Union troops and small detachments of Confederates were by far the most common. More than 7,000 such confrontations are recorded in the *Official Records of the War of the Rebellion.* Most Southern civilians never saw a great battle, but, by 1865, most had encountered some form of raiding party or "irregular" action.

In spite of the huge cost in lives, Grant repeatedly ordered assaults on the Confederate lines, maintaining an unrelenting pressure in an attempt to lure Lee into head-on confrontation.

* U. S. Grant, *Personal Memoirs of Ullyses S. Grant* (New York: Charles M. Webster, 1885), 1: 368.

Time and again, Lee moved away more quickly and established powerful defensive lines. The action moved in an arc east and south as Lee manoeuvred to keep his heavily outnumbered and outgunned army between Richmond and the Federals.

At Spotsylvania Court House on 12th May 1864, the rebels repulsed the Federals in a particularly vicious battle, famous for the intense fighting around the "bloody angle", a U-shaped line of Confederate trenches. "The rebels are piled up in heaps 3 or 4 deep," reported one veteran Massachusetts infantryman. "The pit is filled with them piled up dead and wounded together... I saw one completely trodded in the mud so as to look like part of it and yet he was breathing and gasping." Three weeks later, at Cold Harbor, 7,000 Union troops died in a vain attempt to storm the rebel trenches. "I regret this assault more than any one I have ever ordered," Grant admitted afterwards.[*] It was an eerie harbinger of the futile assaults on the Western Front in the First World War.

By the spring of 1864, two Union soldiers were dying for every Confederate soldier killed. But the North, with more manpower, could stand the losses. At Petersburg, Virginia, in July and August 1864, where Grant's springtime military advance met a final line of entrenchments, the no-man's land between the two armies resembled the

*   Quoted in Shelbey Foote, *Red River to Appomattox*, p. 294.

Somme 50 years later. As on the Somme, troops built supposedly bomb-proof shelters and zigzag trenches. If, at first, soldiers had resisted building proper field fortifications on the grounds that "there was no glory to be gained from fighting out of a hole in the ground", they soon had to accept them as essential.* As one Ohio soldier put it, "the spade is more powerful than the cannon".** Yet the public, the press, and even most military commanders still saw war in terms of knightly heroism and gallant assaults, preferably bayonet charges. The very notion of being able to kill a man without seeing him seemed abhorrent.

Further South, General William Sherman led a force that captured the important strategic city of Atlanta, Georgia at the start of September 1864. Then he led his troops on a notorious march to the Atlantic coast, wreaking destruction. The Union army, Sherman explained, was "not only fighting hostile armies but a hostile people, and must make old and young, rich and poor, feel the hard hand of war". This quote, more than any other, indicates the brutal intent of Union commanders by this late stage of the conflict. In some ways, however, it is misleading. For all its brutality, the Union army never extinguished the distinction between

*   Grady McWhiney and Perry Jamieson, *Attack and Die: Civil War Military Tactics and the Southern Heritage* (University, Alabama: University of Alabama Press, 1982), p. 191.
**   Jerome Mushkat, ed., *A Citizen-Soldier's Civil War: The Letters of Brevet Major General Alvin C. Voris* (Dekalb: Northern Illinois University Press, 2002), p. 192.

soldiers and civilians. When judged by the standards of English efforts to suppress resistance in Ireland, especially under Cromwell – a parallel well known to Civil War generals – or even the campaigns waged against Native Americans at the same time, Sherman's "hard war" doctrine was relatively restrained.

How unified was the South?

The war had a devastating impact on the South. Nearly 40% of white, military-aged men were killed or wounded. The economy was devastated, families torn apart, and a whole way of life destroyed. The scale of the economic crisis facing

McCLELLAN AND THE SEVEN DAYS' BATTLES

In the spring of 1862, the new Union commander, George McClellan, launched what he hoped would be a decisive campaign against the rebels. McClellan was a Democrat, a graduate of the West Point military academy and an accomplished railroad engineer. His press supporters called him the "Little Napoleon", a title that fitted the diminutive, ambitious man very well in every respect except military brilliance or political acumen.

McClellan spent the winter of 1861-2 preparing his enormous army and then, when the dry weather came, floated it to an encampment at the mouth of the James River from where he planned to attack and capture Richmond from the east – an easier approach, he surmised, than marching

the Southern people was quite beyond anything they had imagined when the war began. The paper money issued by the Confederate Treasury was worthless almost as soon as it was printed. Overall, prices multiplied 27 times during the war. Inflation on this scale was useful to the government, insofar as it effectively transferred wealth from ordinary people to the Treasury. But the social strain was enormous.

There were food riots in the streets of towns and cities by 1863, exacerbated by overcrowding from refugees. The most serious public disorder was in Richmond on 2nd April 1863. A crowd shouting "bread or blood" roamed the streets, smashing shop windows and looting food. Jefferson Davis himself appeared to try to calm

overland due south from Washington, over numerous west-east flowing rivers.

There was nothing intrinsically wrong with McClellan's plans but a lot wrong with his ponderous execution. Confederates, given ample warning, were able to counter the Union advance even with inferior numbers. And when the Confederate commander was wounded by Union artillery, he was replaced by Robert Lee, a tactical genius who pushed the Union army back to their original beachhead on the James in a series of devastatingly quick victories known as the Seven Days' Battles.

McClellan has, not unreasonably, been heavily criticised by historians for his timidity – he nagged Washington constantly for reinforcements, perpetually over-estimated the enemy, and seemed strangely reluctant to commit to frontal assaults even when his troops had the advantage. His care with the lives of his men earned him the gratitude of his troops, but

people, but had nothing to offer them other than appeals to patriotism. They dispersed only when threatened by a militia unit.

Yet thousands of letters and diaries attest to the willingness of millions of Southerners to suffer for the cause of independence. Even in the spring of 1865, with Lee's army reduced to a ragged, half-starved rump of its glorious former self, many continued to hope for deliverance from the invaders. When one wealthy Southern woman, Sarah Morgan, was forced to leave Baton Rouge, she was proud to declare:

I have lost my home and all its dear contents for Southern Rights, have stood on its destroyed hearth stone and looked at the ruin of all I loved without a

hobbled his ability to fight a wily, fast-moving general like Lee. In truth, his caution was not wholly the result of a fear of fighting but a product of his politics. Like many Democrats, he was fiercely opposed to secession but equally opposed to emancipation. He wanted to fight a limited war according to the "highest principles of Christian civilization".

His hope was that a massive show of restrained force would be sufficient to demonstrate the seriousness of the Union and would persuade wavering secessionists to rekindle their loyalty. If Southern "property", by which he included slaves, was tampered with, he believed their determination to resist would only be reinforced.

His was a policy which in other times and places would be called winning "hearts and minds". Unfortunately for McClellan, his military failures only reinforced Confederate confidence, while inducing what almost amounted to an inferiority complex in the minds of his own officers. ∎

murmur, almost glad of the sacrifice, if it would contribute its might towards the salvation of the Confederacy.

These sentiments were far from unusual. Had Southerners capitulated sooner they would have suffered much less.

There is evidence of astonishing levels of commitment to the war effort, but also evidence of serious internal division. Which is more telling?

Among the most helpful barometers of morale are the rates of volunteering and desertion from the army. By these measures, Southerners' enthusiasm for continuing the fight for independence was waning by the beginning of 1864. Even by mid-1863, many in the South were realising that a war launched to protect the communities of the South from the menace of black Republicanism had spawned draconian conscription, the impressments of food and other property, the impoverishment of the people and an outbreak of violence and lawlessness. In the wake of the defeat at Gettysburg in July 1863, public meetings were held across the South demanding, in the words of one such meeting in North Carolina, "a speedy, honourable and permanent peace".

When the sacrifices required for victory became too great, families and communities were often put ahead of the "slave owners' republic". In a recent book, *Confederate Reckoning*, Stephanie McCurry has described the great strain the war placed on white women. Forced into unprecedented "public" positions, they exercised considerable power in the wartime South. Towards the end, when they concluded that the Confederate state could not give them security, many effectively withdrew their support for the war, encouraging desertion. McCurry's story of gradual tension and dissolution is, however, not uncontested: Gary Gallagher, in *The Confederate War*, emphasises instead the continuing strength of Confederate loyalty, including among women, who, in at least a few well-documented cases, bore arms to defend their communities when there were no men to do the job for them.

Notwithstanding variations from place to place and through time, the big picture painted by the surviving evidence does seem to indicate a remarkably uniform allegiance to the Southern republic. Only in the final months of the Confederacy did social disorder, banditry, and desertion definitively damage the cause. Clearly, for many, physical privation and loss merely reinforced loyalty.

For four years a Confederate nation-state existed. In some respects it achieved extraordinary feats of organisation, although, in institutional terms, its deficiencies were immense. By 1863 it had lost control of vast swathes of its territory to internal opposition as well as to Union troops. In 1865 it collapsed completely and its elected leaders became hunted outlaws. Yet in its short life the

Confederate States of America inspired fervent loyalty and its eventual failure does not diminish the depths of the popular commitment to it. In the end, it was destroyed by war: it was not an intrinsically fragile entity, bound to fail; nor did the popular nationalism it invoked die when the state collapsed, although inevitably its meaning changed.

How unified was the North?

The short answer is: much less than it was imagined to be in retrospect. Division over emancipation and the conduct of the war went deep. The initial unity after Lincoln's call for troops was severely tested by the price of maintaining a Union, although almost all Northerners, albeit for different reasons, continued to agree it should be maintained.

Public confidence in the prospect of victory reached its lowest ebb in December 1862. The Army of the Potomac suffered more than 12,000 casualties in a futile effort to cross the Rappahannock River in Virginia and take the heavily defended town of Fredericksburg. The debacle earned Union commander Ambrose Burnside the nickname "the butcher of Fredericksburg". "If there is a worse place than Hell, I am in it," Lincoln told a visitor when news came through.

This defeat inaugurated the bleakest period of the war for the North. Advocates of a negotiated peace became more vocal, not only in the Democratic strongholds but in New England and the big eastern cities as well. The prospect of foreign intervention on behalf of the South had receded, but Northern opposition to the war had immeasurably increased. The attempts to recruit men, to sell bonds to fund the war effort, and, above all, to keep up the spirits of the soldiers and their families at home, depended utterly on faith in the possibility of military victory. In the gloomy Christmas of 1862, that prospect dimmed.

The most dramatic manifestation of discontent took place in New York City between 13th and 16th July 1863. In some of the worst rioting in American

PRIVATE WILBUR FISK, 2ND VERMONT VOLUNTEERS

He never rose above the rank of private, yet Wilbur Fisk, a young man who fought almost from the beginning to the end of the war, is one of the thousands who, through their surviving letters, give the Civil War a vividness that most earlier conflicts lack. Fisk's letters were written for publication in his hometown newspaper, but he also kept a private diary, a transcript of which is in the Library of Congress in Washington. And so we know much both about how he wanted to portray himself, and also of his inner uncertainties and self-doubt.

Like hundreds of thousands of other Northerners, Fisk always framed the war as a conflict between democracy and aristocracy. Not a pre-war abolitionist, his letters expressed the common view that slavery taught masters to be tyrants and that slaveholders were trying to

history, thousands of workers, most of them poor Irish immigrants, rampaged through the city in opposition to attempts to implement the draft. They targeted the property of the rich and the offices of Lincoln-supporting newspapers. They also launched indiscriminate attacks on the black population, lynching some, and burning a black orphan asylum.

Their targets reflected their perception that the Republican Party's war was destroying the white man's republic. Order was only restored by troops marching north after the battle of Gettysburg. In retrospect, this was a watershed in the North's Civil War. Mainstream magazines like *Harpers'*

---

subdue the freemen of the North just as they subdued their slaves. In one letter, in September 1863, his wrote what it felt like to be on picket duty in Virginia: "When we reflect that we are standing on the outer verge of all that is left of the American union, and nothing but darkness and rebellion is beyond, and that we are actually guarding our own homes and firesides from treason's usurpations, we feel a thrill of pride that we are permitted to bear a part in maintaining our beloved government." What Fisk was saying was that at stake in the rebellion was that which

made the freedom of his home community possible: the system of "self-rule" and the principle of freedom.

Increasingly, for Fisk as for Lincoln, slavery loomed over the conflict, not just as the mainspring of rebellion, but as a sin for which everyone – Northerners as well as Southerners – had to pay. "The whole nation is involved," he wrote in April 1863, "and deep grief and poignant sorrow must be borne by the North, to expiate the crimes of the South... God does not love slavery; there is no slavery in Heaven. God

contrasted images of rioting, draft-opposing white men with black Union soldiers launching a heroic assault on Fort Wagner. The old race-based conception of citizenship, to which many Northerners still clung, had never faced such a severe challenge.

The Civil War raised troubling questions about whether, in the words of one bestselling pamphlet, a "free people" could "conduct a long war" without sacrificing liberty. Some saw it as an apocalyptic end to free government, whatever the military outcome. These people, strongest in the southern counties of Ohio, Illinois, Indiana, in Western Pennsylvania, and in some of the immigrant

---

does not love rebellion; rebellion could not live there. He hates oppression and oppressors. He loves liberty and respectful obedience to just law."

Yet as his diary reveals, for all the confidence of his public letters, Fisk was besieged by doubts – about his bravery, his faith, and the eventual triumph of his cause. For two months he was even listed as a deserter after he was invalided out and failed to rejoin his regiment, returning home instead to court a women who agreed to marry him. His faith in the righteousness of his cause never deserted him, even if confidence in its eventual success sometimes flickered. Fisk's startlingly articulate descriptions are one reminder that the Civil War was fought by individuals making difficult choices amid all the inconsistencies and uncertainties that we recognise so well from our own lives. ∎

*Hard Marching Every Day: The Civil War Letters of Private Wilbur Fisk, 1861-1865. Edited by Emil and Ruth Rosenblatt. (Lawrence: University Press of Kansas, 1992)

communities of the big cities, tended to be Democrats and to see themselves as the upholders of a long tradition of popular, community-based liberty. They were not, generally speaking, active supporters of the Confederacy, but had become convinced that a military struggle to maintain the Union had been subverted by the "despotic" Lincoln administration into a crusade to liberate the slaves, to enforce racial equality, and to build an Old World-style centralised state. To those opposed to emancipation (at least a third of the northern population), Lincoln was a fanatic who was set on "mongrelising" the white race while subverting the Constitution. Democrats fumed that the administration represented the "persecuting, intolerant, hateful and malignant... Puritan spirit of New England".

For a group of elite businessmen, editors and ministers, however, the war offered an opportunity to forge a new nationalism and to reassert the value of respect for constituted authority. These men – mostly Republicans and anti-slavery activists – believed that while the war was the product of slavery, it was also a symptom of moral and political decay. Large-scale Catholic Irish immigration had challenged their conception of a Protestant republic, and the booming cities threatened the kind of class conflict that they associated with Europe. They hoped the war would stimulate a disciplined, patriotic republican citizenry who would exercise their freedom responsibly, deferring to society's "natural" leaders.

In spite of internal conflict, no one ever suggested suspending elections for the duration of the war; they were, after all, the practical manifestation of popular government for which the war was being fought. But elections, which mixed carnival, evangelical revival meeting, gang violence and melodramatic on-stage posturing, brought conflict to the surface. Arguing that support for the administration was nothing less than a patriotic duty, mass-membership Union Leagues mobilised voters across the North – and intimidated opponents, sometimes with threats of violence. Lincoln and his political supporters regarded Republican victories in wartime elections as no less than an extension of the battle being fought against Confederate armies.

Political conflict within the North came to a head in the November 1864 presidential election. Lincoln's re-election was more important to the outcome of the war than any individual battle. Had he lost, the result would, rightly, have been interpreted by the Confederates as a sign that the Northern will was fatally weakened. Democrats appealed to Northerners' sense of anger and despair at the cost of the war; Lincoln appealed to their determination to finish the job. In the end, the president won re-election, but not by so big a majority as might be imagined, and with plenty of evidence of soldiers being intimidated into supporting him.

Civil War victory papered over the cracks, as victory always does. In May 1865 a grand review of the Union armies in Washington D.C. was a triumphant celebration of the endurance of the core values that almost all Northerners could endorse – that the Union, now preserved in its territorial integrity, was the guarantor of self-government. The grand review marked the rapid demobilisation of most of the million-strong army that had defeated the rebels. For the moment the impending difficulties of integrating a formerly enslaved population into the polity could be forgotten.

When and how did the war end?

To all intents and purposes, the war ended on 9th April 1865. That, at least, was the perception of most Americans, North and South, at the time. At the beginning of the month, Robert Lee, the Confederate General, had been forced to abandon his defences outside Petersburg, the gateway to Richmond, where he had held off Union forces for nine months. On 2nd April, in anticipation of the fall of Petersburg, the Confederate government abandoned Richmond, setting it aflame before President Davis and his cabinet fled west. The following day, the Confederate capital, one of the principal objectives of four years of warfare, was in Union hands. In emotional scenes, the black population of Richmond cheered Abraham Lincoln and strained to touch him when, against the advice of those worried about assassination, he visited the still-smouldering city and sat quietly for a moment behind Davis's desk in the recently abandoned "Confederate White House".

Meanwhile, the half-starved remnants of the Army of Northern Virginia, now grossly outnumbered by the Army of the Potomac, were chased into the remote far southwest corner of Virginia. On 8th April, Union cavalry overtook Lee's army and captured two trainloads of desperately needed rations. Lee and his men had finally come to the end of the road. The following day, Lee formally surrendered his army at Appomattox Courthouse, a tiny hamlet in Southwest Virginia.

Grant and Lee met in the drawing room of a private home belonging to a man named Wilmer McLean. Four years earlier, McLean had been farming near Manassas, Virginia, when the first battle of the war had been fought on his land. He sold up and moved to the far southwest of the state. Now, in one of those ironic coincidences that would be unbelievable in fiction, he found himself playing host to the war's last rites. For a few minutes the two generals exchanged pleasantries. Then Lee brought them to the business at hand. Grant wrote out the surrender terms and Lee

Vivien Leigh playing the Southern belle, Scarlett O'Hara, in the 1939 film Gone With the Wind.

signed them.

Grant had no mandate to determine the form the peace would take in a constitutional or legal sense when he sat down with Lee. He was empowered by Lincoln simply to accept the surrender of the Confederate army under Lee's command and nothing more. Nevertheless, the agreement established a powerful template for post-war reconciliation. On the one hand, Grant promised Lee that his men would be "paroled" – not "disturbed by United States authority", still less imprisoned, or prosecuted – on condition that they obeyed the laws and did not take up arms again. On the other hand, Lee thanked his men for their sacrifices, made the important and reassuring observation that they had been defeated in the end only because they were overwhelmingly outnumbered, and urged them to go home and be peaceful citizens of the United States.

The agreement at Appomattox closed off one possible alternative: that Lee could have ordered his men to resist the invading armies as small guerrilla bands. One of Lee's artillery officers suggested this move on the morning of 9th April. He dismissed the idea, warning that in response the Union army would simply step up their war against the infrastructure and civilians of the South. In any case, if the South no longer had a functioning civilian authority, what would they be fighting for?

Strictly speaking, Appomattox was not the end of the war. Other Confederate forces were still undefeated. General Joseph Johnston, commanding three times as many Confederate troops as Lee, was still at large – he surrendered two weeks later. General Kirby Smith, commander of Confederate forces west of the Mississippi finally surrendered at Galveston, Texas on 2nd June. Meanwhile, the civilian leader of the rebels, Jefferson Davis, remained a fugitive when Lee surrendered: he was still flinging out orders as if he still had power, and had no intention of conceding defeat. He was captured on 10th May in Georgia.

Yet, overwhelmingly, white Southerners – even those who had pledged to die rather than accept the authority of the United States – saw Appomattox as the end. "'It is useless to struggle longer,' seems to be the common cry," one Georgia woman wrote, on hearing the news. "The poor wounded men go hobbling about the streets with despair on their faces. There is a new pathos in a crutch or an empty sleeve, now, that we know it was all for nothing." When the news reached Florida another female diarist could only write that "the very earth had crumbled beneath our feet". In the North, too, news of Lee's surrender was regarded as the effective end of the rebellion. The streets of Northern cities were covered in patriotic bunting and families looked forward to the imminent return of their menfolk in the army.

Why should the surrender of one army, Lee's, be treated as the end of the conflict? The answer lies in the political and moral stature that Lee himself had acquired, as well as in the strategic significance of having finally captured the Confederate capital. Appomattox was the end because Lee made it so. The man in whom Southern hopes had been invested, who had a near-Godlike status never remotely equalled by any political leader in the South, had effectively called an end to the war. And so the war ended.

The assassination of President Lincoln less than a week after Appomattox threatened to turn the course of the war once more – not back in favour of the South (though many imagined the act was a last desperate bid for independence by Jefferson Davis) but, because of the outraged calls for vengeance, in favour of a far harsher military subjugation of the South than had been envisaged in Wilmer McLean's quiet rural home.

In the end, the Confederacy sank fast. Ever since the fall of Atlanta – a big strategic railroad hub – at the start of September 1864, it had been hard to see how the ever-growing Union forces could fail to destroy the rapidly-depleting Confederate troops.

But the resilience of the South was extraordinary. Until Lee was forced to abandon Richmond, white Southerners – despite a localised peace movement, bread riots, and political turmoil – had been willing to throw everything they had at the invaders. In its dying days, the Confederate Congress even passed a law which would have emancipated slaves who were thereafter to be enlisted in the Confederate army. Ironically, this was the one move that – had it been done at the start of the war – would very likely have secured Southern independence. Yet there were plenty of Southerners who, upon hearing of the Confederate "emancipation", concluded that they may as well end the suffering and surrender, since the cause was thereby already lost.

For slaveholders (and about a third of the 1860 white population in the South had at least some financial investment in slavery), the final months of the war and its immediate aftermath were especially shocking, their confident vision of a slave-based, modern republic shattered. Those who had always boasted of the loyalty and even the love of their slave "family" found that enslaved people actively supported the destruction of the rebellion. Although the majority of slaves did not run away, masters were suddenly profoundly uncertain about the loyalty of those who remained.

The apparent arbitrariness of slaves' behaviour was particularly disconcerting: especially favoured slaves, such as house servants, mammies and drivers, might leave without a word, while those with a reputation as "bad niggers" remained. Many whites observed with bewilderment that the slaves of benevolent masters were as likely to desert as those of harsh owners. The wife of a Presbyterian minister in Georgia wrote that she was "thoroughly disgusted with the whole race".

Why did the South lose?

General Lee offered an answer to this question after his surrender at Appomattox. "After four years of arduous service, marked by unsurpassed courage and fortitude," he told his men, "the Army of Northern Virginia has been compelled to yield to overwhelming numbers and resources." In the years after the Civil War, white Southerners followed his cue, telling an emotionally powerful story of a heroic and noble struggle against overwhelming odds.

If Lee was right, historians need not look south of the Mason-Dixon line to explain the war's outcome: the answer is simply the old story of the biggest battalions winning. And that was certainly how things looked in the bitter final year of the war, when the armies of Grant and Sherman vastly outnumbered and outgunned the Confederates. The North clearly had advantages that, in the end, were brought to bear.

But Lee's explanation was too simple. Americans, after all, could draw on their own history for lessons in the possibility of establishing an independent nation through war. Like their Revolutionary forebears in their struggle against the mighty British army, the Confederates could have won against superior odds because they had compensating advantages: a resilient population, talented military leaders, the advantage of fighting a defensive war in country they knew, and, above all, a cause for which the vast majority of white Southerners were prepared to make great sacrifices.

If this was so, then the causes of Confederate defeat were, in part, internal rather than external – the political divisions that beset the Confederacy, for example. According to this view, the Confederacy was hoist by its own petard: its devotion to decentralised government, endless checks on executive power, and obsession with individual liberty undermined its unity and capacity to fight. Perhaps, in the historian David Donald's striking phrase, the South "died of democracy".

Confederate President Jefferson Davis certainly faced plenty of opposition – but then so too did Lincoln. And what is more striking about the Confederacy is how much power the government in Richmond had, taking control of the railroads and munitions manufacturing, and impounding property – including slaves – if it was deemed essential to the war effort. From nothing, the South created what was for a while one of the most effective and disciplined armies the world had seen.

Perhaps, then, the underlying failure of the Confederacy can be found in fault lines in Southern society. Did class tensions between slaveholding and non-slaveholding whites undermine the war effort? Were women on the home front insufficiently committed to the cause? In fact, only in the final months, when Union military superiority became invincible, did a failure of morale tangibly affect the ability of Confederate armies to resist. This was a resilient society prepared to make huge sacrifices.

The most convincing internal factor behind Southern defeat was the very institution that prompted secession in the first place: slavery. Enslaved people used the war to flee when they could. More than a hundred thousand ended up in Union army uniform. Nevertheless, without the incursions of the Union army and the collapsing capacity of the Confederacy to resist, slavery would probably not in itself have defeated the South. Slavery helped destroy the South primarily because of the incursions of the Union army, just as military defeats were often the cause of political division rather than the other way around.

If weaknesses in Southern society don't completely explain Confederate defeat, does that return us to Lee's explanation at Appommatox – that the North was simply too strong? In a sense, yes, but with a crucial caveat: so long as the North remained determined to crush the rebellion by force, it was always likely that their superiority in manpower and resources would tell in the end.

But would the North remain willing to pay the high price of victory? The Confederates certainly

LINCOLN'S ASSASSINATION

Had Mr and Mrs Lincoln not gone to the theatre on Good Friday, 14th April 1865, not only would the aftermath of the Civil War have been different, but we would remember the war, and its principal leader, quite differently today. Lincoln was assassinated at the moment of his greatest triumph.

The streets of Washington had been decorated in patriotic bunting, celebrating the surrender of General Lee the previous Monday. On Tuesday, Lincoln had given a speech from a balcony of the White House to a cheering crowd in which he had, for the first time, suggested that some black men – at least those who had served in the Union army – should be given the vote.

understood the centrality of this question. Lee and Davis knew the North had more men and more industrial capacity, so they tried to attack their enemies where they were most vulnerable – popular commitment to the cause. Events on the battlefield mattered at least as much for their impact on home front morale as on the strategic position of the armies. The North won the war because the idea of maintaining the Union was powerful enough to overcome any doubts. Here, Lincoln played a role with his speeches, but so too did countless newspaper editors, clergymen, anti-slavery speakers, and ordinary families talking about why the rebellion had to be crushed.

The North could very well have lost the war, but only if it had lost the will to win. And despite

In the crowd that evening was John Wilkes Booth, one of the leading Shakespearean actors of the day. A man of strong Southern sympathies, he had been collecting an oddball crew of misfits and criminals with the intention of enacting a final, melodramatic act of revenge and catharsis.

Perhaps Lincoln's heretical support for black rights crystallised Booth's determination to kill the man he regarded as a tyrant. No doubt also, the public announcement that the president would visit Ford's Theatre that Friday gave him an irresistible stage on which to carry out his plan.

Our American Cousin was being staged that week, a play based on a script by the prolific British writer Tom Taylor, but which a touring New York theatre company had turned into a comedy of manners lampooning English aristocratic pretension. Booth had the advantage of knowing the play as well as the theatre.

wobbles, they never did. The point was tellingly made by Alvin C. Voris, an officer in the 67th Ohio Infantry. "It is not so much the capacity to win battles" that gives victory to a people, he mused in a letter to his wife, as "the ability to bear grief".

Conclusion

"The lie of the Civil War," the African American scholar and activist Ta-Nehisi Coates wrote, "is the lie of innocence." He meant the myths that obscure the violence and injustices of that great conflict and what it represented: the theft of the lives of millions of black people on which American prosperity and the embedded privileges of

Slipping in through a side door, he waited outside the presidential box for the line in the play that was guaranteed to draw the biggest laugh: "I know enough to turn you inside out, old gal – you sockdologizing old man-trap!"

As the audience were convulsed, he stepped behind the president, shot him in the head and leaped to the stage, shouting, according to some reports "sic semper tyrannis" ("thus always to tyrants"). Perhaps no other world leader has been killed while hundreds of his supporters were laughing.

Several moments went by before the audience began to realise what had happened, as the screams from Mary Lincoln overpowered the hilarity.

Lincoln didn't die instantly, but he never regained consciousness. He was taken across the road to a boarding house where he died the following morning. His assassin was killed while on the run. Some of his confederates were hanged. One had attempted to

"whiteness" have been founded. Coates is right that there was nothing innocent about this war – it happened because a group of powerful men were willing to break up the United States in order to try to preserve a violent system of forced labour and racial oppression.

This was a conflict with origins deeply embedded in the American past, yet we should never lose sight of the fact that war was a choice, not a historical inevitability. It was a choice made by men (and, within the limits of a patriarchal political system, women too) who, with varying degrees of conviction, preferred mass violence to the alternatives. And nor was there just a single moment of choice but many, because although we use the singular, "*the* war", this was an evolving multi-

---

murder Secretary of State Seward the same night but had succeeded only in wounding him.

Just as the audience in Ford's Theatre had lurched, bewildered, from laughter to shock, so the North as a whole was confronted by an unimaginable outrage just at the moment of national celebration. Lincoln, a divisive figure in life, hated by his political opponents in the North as passionately as he had been loved by his supporters, was swiftly canonised – the embodiment of all that the Union had been struggling for.

That he was shot on Good Friday – seemingly giving his life that the nation might live – was a symbolism not lost on the ministers who addressed weeping congregations on Easter Sunday. That the president had been shot in a theatre – still regarded askance by many in this Puritan-influenced country – rather spoiled the narrative, but most managed to overlook it. ∎

layered conflict in which at various stages decisions had to be made about whether and how to carry it forward.

There were choices to be made at the close of the conflict too. Lincoln had died having sketched out only the vaguest outlines of a plan for post-war Reconstruction. It was left to his successor, Andrew Johnson, to deal with the aftermath. For 150 years there has been a cottage industry of people imagining how the history of post-war America might have been different if Lincoln had lived on. White Southerners who had execrated him when he was alive turned him, in the late 19th century, into an unlikely fallen champion of moderation. After all, had he not promised in his second inaugural address that his policy would be guided by "malice toward none, charity for all"? And when he had made decisions as president about how to restore Union-supporting governments in parts of the Confederacy that were occupied by US troops, such as Louisiana and Arkansas, he had spurned the advice of radicals in his own party and favoured conciliating white Southern moderates who might form the nucleus of loyal post-war governments.

Yet Lincoln had also speculated about enfranchising black men, a proposal regarded as terrifying by even the most moderate Southerner in 1865. The ambiguity about what Lincoln might have done reflected the twin poles of Reconstruction politics. On the one hand, Reconstruction was about stability – ensuring that there was no return to rebellion, fear of which, with the benefit of hindsight, is all too easy to underestimate. Maintaining stability required bringing the South back into a "normal" relationship with the rest of the country as quickly as possible while reassuring Southerners that the end of slavery need not mean the end of economic prosperity or social order.

On the other hand, Reconstruction raised expectations of, and demands for, justice: justice for those who had risked their lives for the Union, and for those families which had suffered so many generations of enslavement. There were plenty of people – radical Republican leaders like Senator Charles Sumner, for example – who argued that there was no tension between these goals because only a just peace would be a lasting one. But justice for African Americans meant provoking continuing violent opposition from the majority white community, so in practice stability and justice remained stubbornly hard to reconcile.

Lincoln's successor, Andrew Johnson, was a Southerner from Tennessee. He was a Unionist, of course, and had been selected as Lincoln's running mate in the 1864 election in order to broaden Lincoln's appeal, to give substance to the idea that he was not a merely a "sectional" leader but a genuinely national one. No one expected Johnson to become president – vice presidents are rarely selected on that basis. And his accidental elevation to the White House created a bizarre situation in which a man whose every instinct and experience was in tune with the white South – albeit as a vociferous opponent of secession – ended up having to work with a Republican-dominated Congress determined to impose a lasting, radical settlement on the defeated South.

Johnson's approach to Reconstruction was to let white Southerners run their states again as soon as possible, with only two provisos: that they accepted the letter of the Thirteenth Amendment, abolishing slavery, and renounced secession. Goaded by Johnson's intransigence, Congress pushed for, and eventually implemented, a much more radical programme, involving a very light-touch military occupation of the former Confederacy and, more importantly, the passage of two further constitutional amendments that gave equal citizenship to black people (or, more specifically, to anyone born in the United States).

Equal citizenship meant, at least in theory, that if one of the "privileges" of white citizenship was to vote, that right could not be denied to black people either. If white people were given free elementary schooling, or were expected to serve on juries, or could be elected to office, or could own property under the laws of their state, blacks could not be denied the same – in law, at least, they could not be denied these things *on the grounds of race.*

The years from about 1867 to about 1876 were known to generations of American school children – in one of the greatest and most pernicious of the lies that Ta-Nehisi Coates refers to – as the years of "black Reconstruction" or, in the words of a (white) Southern historian writing in the 1930s, the "Tragic Era".

For a brief time, the presence of US troops made a reality of black political participation. African Americans were elected in substantial numbers to local and state bodies, including the US Senate. For a few months, even South Carolina had a black governor. But the bi-racial electoral coalitions that governed the ex-Confederate states for these few years were brought down, one by one, by extra-legal violence. The Ku Klux Klan is only the most famous of the white supremacist groups that staged what amounted to an armed uprising to overthrow these Reconstruction governments, "redeeming" their states, as they put it, from the unholy indignity of black people having been granted power.

We cannot begin to understand the racial politics of the United States in the 20th and 21st centuries without understanding the Civil War, that still-echoing explosion of violence driven by America's everlasting problem with race. The Fourteenth Amendment's guarantees of black citizenship were, of course, ignored in practice until the 1950s at the earliest, but they meant that Martin Luther King could say, with justice, that if the cause of Civil Rights was wrong, the "Constitution of the United States is wrong". In America's perpetual conversation about race, all roads really do lead back to the Civil War.

The aftermath of the Civil War was not just felt in the former Confederacy. From Appomattox, the pathways of US history lead us west – to the mechanised destruction of Native American resistance, to the building of the transcontinental railroads and to the constant flow of people and financial investment towards the Pacific. The late 19th and early 20th centuries saw both the consolidation of the monopoly power of nation-states and the increasing interconnectedness of the globe, and, in America, the aftermath of the war saw the rise of massive corporations and the spread of industrial capitalism on a scale that Lincoln's generation could never have imagined. So while the world the South went to war to defend was buried forever, so too, in a sense, was the small-scale capitalism that Northerners assumed to be the only alternative to a slave-based economy.

A hundred and fifty years after Appomattox, there is no settled, singular "meaning" to the American Civil War. It remains contested territory, a formative eruption in the creation of what we think of as the "modern" world, a source of fascination in the way it leads us, if we study it with our eyes open, away from innocent stories to the darker, brutal, uncompromising realities that, then and now, shape how men and women live and imagine their world.

CHRONOLOGY OF KEY EVENTS

Major battles are highlighted in **bold**

1820 Missouri Compromise prohibits future expansion of slavery into United States territories north of the 36'30° line of latitude.

1833 Slavery abolished in the British Empire.
Formation of American Anti-Slavery Society.

1844 Democrat James K. Polk narrowly wins Presidential election.

1846-1847 Mexican War brings vast new territories into the United States.
David Wilmot introduces a proviso which would ban slavery from new territories sparking political crisis over slavery expansion.

1848 Formation of Free Soil Party.
Whig Zachary Taylor elected president.

1850 Taylor dies and is succeeded by Millard Fillmore.
Compromise measures passed by Congress to settle status of slavery in Mexican cession.

1852 Democrat Franklin Pierce elected President.

1854 Kansas-Nebraska Act rescinds the Missouri Compromise and reopens slavery controversy.

1856 Charles Sumner attacked in Senate.

Kansas in state of civil war.
Democrat James Buchanan elected president.

1857 Dred Scott decision.

1858 Lincoln-Douglas debates in Illinois.

1859 John Brown's raid on Harpers Ferry.

1860 Nov 6 Lincoln elected president.
Dec 20 South Carolina legislature votes for secession.

1861 Jan 9 – Feb 1 Secession of Mississippi, Florida,
Alabama, Georgia, Louisiana and Texas.
Mar 4 Lincoln inaugurated.
Mar 11 Montgomery convention approves Confederate
constitution.
Apr 12-13 Bombardment and surrender of Fort Sumter.
Apr 17-May 20 Secession of Virginia, Arkansas, Tennessee
and North Carolina.
May 13 British government declares neutrality.
May 20 Kentucky declares neutrality.
July 21 Confederate victory at Bull Run.
Sept 3-6 End of Kentucky's "neutrality".
Nov-Dec Trent crisis.

**1862 Feb 6-25 Union capture of Forts Henry and
Donelson** on Tennessee River.
Mar 6 Lincoln proposes gradual emancipation to Congress.
Mar 17 – Apr 2 McClellan moves Army of the Potomac to
James River for Peninsular Campaign.
Apr 6-7 Grant turns near-defeat into victory at Shiloh.
Apr 16 Confederate Congress passes Conscription Act.
Apr 24-25 New Orleans occupied by Union.
June 1 Lee takes command of Army of Northern Virginia.

June 26-July 2 Lee drives McClellan back from Richmond in Seven Days' battles.

July 22 Lincoln reads draft of Emancipation Proclamation to cabinet.

Aug 27 Bragg leads Confederate invasion of Kentucky.

Aug 29-30 Confederate victory at Second Bull Run.

Sept 4 Lee invades Maryland.

Sept 17 Battle of Antietam, followed by Lee's withdrawal into Virginia.

Sept 22 Preliminary Emancipation Proclamation issued.

Oct-Nov Republicans lose seats in Congressional mid-term elections.

Dec 13 Union defeat at Battle of Fredericksburg.

Dec 31-Jan 1 Battle of Stones River followed by Bragg's withdrawal.

1863 Jan 1 Emancipation Proclamation issued.

Mar 3 Conscription Act passed by US Congress.

Apr 2 Bread riot in Richmond.

Apr 24 Confederate Congress imposes sweeping new taxes.

Apr 30-May 6 Lee routs Hooker's Army of the Potomac at Chancellorsville.

May 10 Death of "Stonewall" Jackson.

June 3 Lee invades North.

July 1-3 Union victory at Gettysburg followed by Lee's withdrawal.

July 4 Vicksburg falls to Grant after long campaign.

July 13-16 New York City draft riots.

Nov 19 Lincoln delivers Gettysburg Address.

Nov 24-25 Union victory at Chattanooga opens way for Union invasion of Georgia.

1864 Feb Confederate Congress passes series of tough new laws on tax, impressments and suspension of habeas corpus.

Mar 9 Grant becomes general-in-chief of all Union

armies.

Apr 12 Massacre of black Union troops at Fort Pillow.

May 5-6 Battle of the Wilderness.

May 8-21 Battles at Spotsylvania Court House.

June 1-3 Battle of Cold Harbor.

June 7 Lincoln re-nominated by Baltimore Convention of the National Union Party.

June 15-18 Attacks on Petersburg, beginning of siege.

July 11 Confederate raid led by Jubal E. Early threatens Washington.

July 30 Battle of the Crater.

Sept 2 Sherman captures Atlanta after long campaign through Georgia.

Oct 19 Union victory at Cedar Creek ends Confederate threat in Shenandoah Valley.

Nov 8 Lincoln re-elected president.

Nov 15 Sherman begins march to the sea.

Dec 21 Savannah falls to Sherman.

1865 Jan 31 US Congress passes Thirteenth Amendment abolishing slavery.

Feb 17 Confederates evacuate Charleston.

Mar 4 Lincoln's second inauguration.

Mar 13 Confederate Congress authorises recruitment of slaves into army.

Apr 2 Fall of Petersburg.

Apr 3 Fall of Richmond.

Apr 9 Lee surrenders to Grant at Appomattox Court House.

Apr 14 Lincoln shot by John Wilkes Booth, dies next morning.

Apr 26 General Johnston surrenders in North Carolina.

May 10 Jefferson Davis captured in Georgia.

May 26 Surrender of General Kirby Smith in west brings war formally to an end.

BIBLIOGRAPHY

In the last few years, the key books that have been re-shaping the field of Civil War studies include James Oakes' *Freedom National* (2013), which makes the case that the North was far more committed to antislavery politics than previous historians have thought, and Ed Baptist, *The Half Has Never Been Told* (2014), which shows how slavery was central to US economic growth – in the North as well as the South – in the 19th century.

A very different perspective from Oakes's is Gary Gallagher's *The Union War* (2011). He argues that Northerners were motivated by their vision of the Union and not by antislavery politics per se. Andre Fleche's *The Revolution of 1861* (2012) places secession and the war for the Union in the context of the European Revolutions of 1848 and their aftermath, while Robert May's book, *Slavery, Race and Conquest in the Tropics* (2013) emphasises the importance of Caribbean and Latin American expansionism in generating the crisis.

On the wartime experience of Northerners, William Blair's new book *With Malice Towards Some* (2014) discusses how issues of loyalty were debated, while Stephanie McCurry's *Confederate Reckoning* (2011) argues that the Confederacy was undermined from within by tensions over gender as well as slavery. One of the best of the many biographies of Lincoln is by Richard J. Carwardine, *Lincoln: a Life of Purpose and Power* (2006). Good overviews of the war include James M. McPherson, *Battle Cry of Freedom* (1988) and Adam I. P. Smith, *The American Civil War* (2007).

ℭℊ CONNELL GUIDES

MORE IN OUR NEW HISTORY SERIES

"Connell Guides should be required reading in every school in the country."
Julian Fellowes, creator of Downton Abbey

"What Connell Guides do is bring immediacy and clarity: brevity with depth. They unlock the complex and offer students an entry route."
Colin Hall, Head of Holland Park School

"These guides are a godsend. I'm so glad I found them."
Jessica Enthoven, A Level student, St Mary's Calne

"Completely brilliant. I wish I were young again with these by my side. It's like being in a room with marvellous tutors. You can't really afford to be without them, and they are a joy to read."
Joanna Lumley

To buy any of these guides, or for more information, go to
www.connellguides.com
Or contact us on (020)79932644 / info@connellguides.com

LITERATURE GUIDES

Novels and poetry
Emma
Far From the Madding Crowd
Frankenstein
Great Expectations
Hard Times
Heart of Darkness
Jane Eyre
Lord of the Flies
Mansfield Park
Middlemarch
Mrs Dalloway
Paradise Lost
Persuasion
Pride and Prejudice
Tess of the D'Urbervilles
The Canterbury Tales
The Great Gatsby
The Poetry of Robert Browning
The Waste Land
To Kill A Mockingbird
Wuthering Heights

Shakespeare
A Midsummer Night's Dream
Antony and Cleopatra
Hamlet
Julius Caesar
King Lear
Macbeth
Othello
Romeo and Juliet
The Second Tetralogy
The Tempest
Twelfth Night

Modern texts
A Doll's House
A Room with a View
A Streetcar Named Desire
An Inspector Calls
Animal Farm
Atonement
Beloved
Birdsong
Hullabaloo
Never Let Me Go
Of Mice and Men
Rebecca
Spies
The Bloody Chamber
The Catcher in the Rye
The History Boys
The Road
Vernon God Little
Waiting for Godot

NEW
A Short History of English
Literature
American literature
Dystopian literature

How to read a poem
How to read Shakespeare
The Gothic
The poetry of Christina Rossetti
Women in literature

INDEX

First published in 2017 by
Connell Guides
Spye Arch House
Spye Park
Lacock
Wiltshire
SN15 2PR

10 9 8 7 6 5 4 3 2 1

A CIP catalogue record for this book is available from the British Library.
ISBN 978-1-911187-25-7

Picture credits:

p.95 © Selznick/MGM/REX/Shutterstock

Design © Nathan Burton

Assistant Editors and typeset by:
Brian Scrivener and Paul Woodward

www.connellguides.com

Printed and bound by CPI Group (UK) Ltd, Croydon, CR0 4YY